D1121827

Gunpowder

…enough, wee possessed…

…lizabeth.

…all persons that…

horrible conspiracie…

Guido Fawkes

Gunpowder

The Players behind the Plot

JAMES TRAVERS

the national archives

For Romilly

First published in 2005 by
The National Archives
Kew, Richmond
Surrey, TW9 4DU, UK
www.nationalarchives.gov.uk

The National Archives (TNA)
was formed when the
Public Record Office (PRO)
and Historical Manuscripts
Commission (HMC)
combined in April 2003.

A catalogue card for this book
is available from the
British Library.

ISBN 1 903365 86 4

ENDPAPERS
The Middlesex county inquisition
as to the goods of Gunpowder Plot
conspirator Sir Everard Digby,
attainted 1609–10. The valuable items
listed include a bedstead, curtains,
bolster and valance claimed by
Sir William Waad in lieu of 'necessaries'
supplied to Digby when imprisoned
in the Tower (E 178/4179).

FRONTISPIECE
Guy Fawkes's signature
(SP 14/216/f.152b)

Edited by Catherine Bradley
Designed by Ken Wilson

Printed in the UK
by Butler and Tanner,
Frome, Somerset

Contents

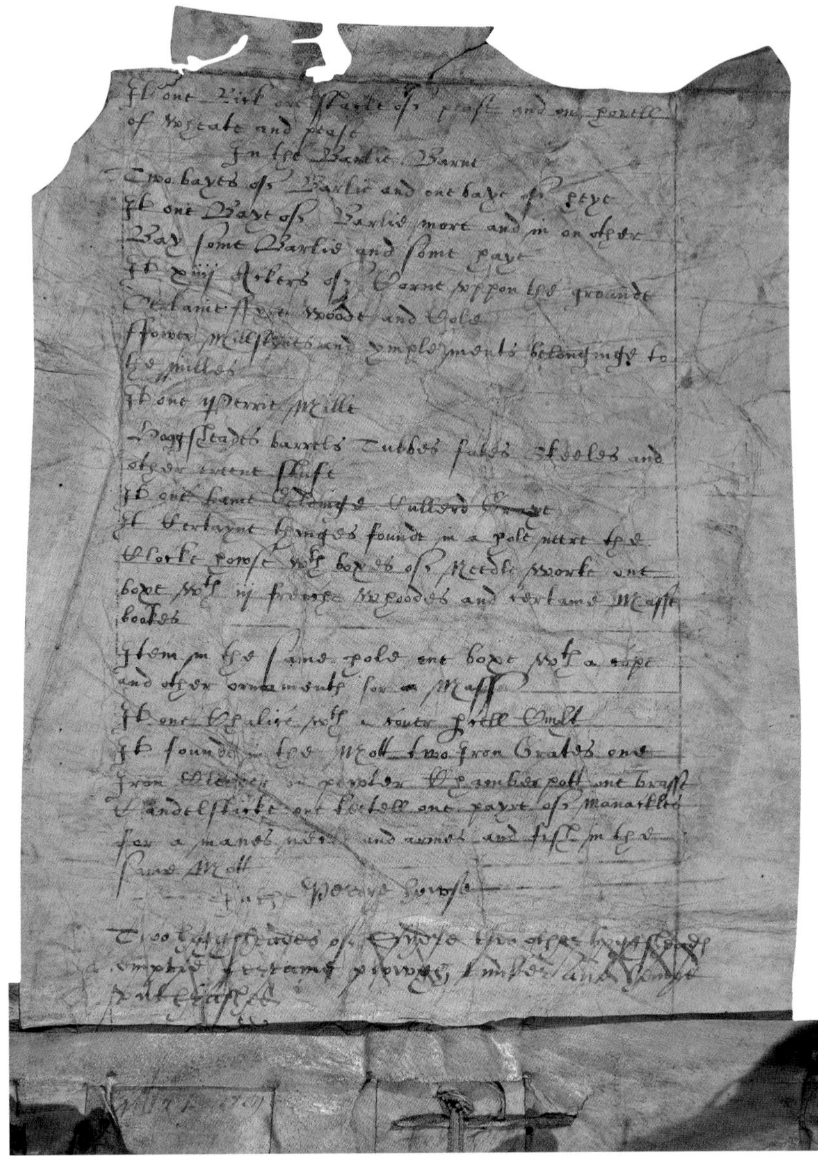

A SUFFOLK county inquisition as to the possessions of Ambrose Rookwood, a Gunpowder Plot conspirator (above), noted 'Item: certain things found in a hole near the clock house with boxes of needlework, one box with 3 French hoods and certain mass books. Item: in the same hole one box with a cope and other ornaments for a mass.' Many aspects of the hidden religious life of English Catholics were revealed by investigations into the plot (E 178/4006).
A contemporary German engraving (right) of the Gunpowder Plot conspirators.

The Argument

THE THING that strikes you about this famous group engraving of the Gunpowder Plotters is their social ease. True, there is a certain amount of whispering and passing of notes, but overall they look like a group of men at a wine and cheese party whose only conspiracy has been not to invite their wives so that they can tell risqué jokes. Are they simply being represented as bad plotters, too good-humoured and gregarious to keep treason to themselves? Or is there a hidden truth in this image about the nature of the plot, one that helps to explain its unending controversy? This book explores the complex characters behind the plot, not as automata driven by inexorable historical forces discernible only with hindsight, but as social beings whose fates were determined by key moments, which we can reconstruct from documents held at The National Archives and elsewhere.

This book also presents a wider perspective on the Gunpowder Plot and the individuals it enveloped. It follows the small group of plotters pictured here beyond the whispering London world, where the conspiracy to blow up the House of Lords was hatched, to a house on the borders of Worcestershire and Staffordshire where they accidentally blew themselves up with their own gunpowder. It traces the rippling repercussions of the plot, from local loyalties and law enforcement in England to the machinations of international politics. The engraving shows the core plotters, those who dominated and drove the scheme forwards: Robert Catesby, gentleman, of Ashby St Ledgers, Northamptonshire, who was its mastermind; Thomas Percy, gentleman, constable of Alnwick Castle, member of the king's bodyguard and the group's means of access to Parliament and the royal family; and Thomas Wintour, gentleman, soldier and scholar, its diplomatic arm who in Flanders had recruited Guy Fawkes – a man skilled in arms who had served Spanish forces abroad for so long that his face was conveniently unknown in England. John Wright, another core conspirator and a schoolfellow of Fawkes in York, is shown listening, while Catesby and Percy talk simultaneously. He seems to have been the strong and silent type. Both Wright and Thomas Wintour recruited their brothers as extra manpower, and both are depicted on the edge of the group. Robert Wintour, the elder brother who had inherited the family estate in Worcestershire, is shown in a worldly way passing a note to Catesby's servant Thomas Bate; characteristically, he is looking outside the group to his responsibilities beyond.

Many more players behind the plot lurk in the shadows around this social circle. The late rich recruits, Sir Everard Digby, Ambrose Rookwood and Francis Tresham, are all still to arrive at the party – indeed, Catesby seems barely to have introduced them to the others before the plot was discovered. Lord Monteagle, Tresham's brother-in-law, hailed as the saviour of his nation for disclosing an anonymous letter warning of the plot, had employed Thomas Wintour as his secretary and had been in plotters' circles for years. Henry Percy, Earl of Northumberland, Thomas Percy's cousin who had appointed the plotter to the king's bodyguard, was reportedly already dissatisfied with the Scottish king he had done so much to bring to the English throne. Henry Garnet, Father Superior of the English Jesuit Province, was close to the core plotters, but was he a restraining influence or the arch-plotter himself? Deeper in the shadows, were this happy group monitored and manipulated even as they spoke by their intended victims, the principal secretary of state Robert Cecil, Earl of Salisbury, and the king himself?

In writing the history of something as controversial as the

Gunpowder Plot, characters can swiftly become polarized on ideological grounds. But original documents generally show them as much more ambiguous, human and interesting. Certainly the conspirators appear with a more human face and complex character than the official version of events would allow, but this also makes them more difficult to excuse or dismiss as simply pawns in a fabrication. The great ideological divide between religious groups is real and ever-present, but as you study a key moment in the plot it is often unclear exactly where each character stands in relation to this great divide – and still less clear whether any character's position remains constant as you go on. That ambiguity and playfulness with language which makes their contemporary William Shakespeare's 'position' on almost any subject notoriously difficult to establish was not confined to him, though perhaps he did it with the greatest skill. It was a broader cultural phenomenon, evolving in response to political and religious uncertainties, and the players behind the plot used the same type of language even *in extremis*. Generally there are more interpretations possible than historians usually admit. Contemporaries described the Gunpowder Plot as a tragedy, but it is one made all the more tense, exciting and terrible by the fact that the dead bodies on the stage at the end of the final act are real.

Unlike the well-crafted drama of the period with its inexorable dramatic irony, real events unfolded in a fragmentary way without modern conveniences in bureaucracy or reportage to inform or co-ordinate. We shall see the government use torture to gain information which was in their hands a hundred miles away. For much of the first week after the discovery of the plot, the official investigation was a frantic attempt to gain information about a rebellion which was over almost before they knew of it. Local information could be accurate as far as it went, but it was often overlooked or superseded before it was known. The government was reliant for law enforcement on local gentry, characters who were not unlike the plotters themselves, so there was always the possibility that, however clearly worded your proclamation, nothing would actually happen on the ground.

The scenes of the plot divide naturally into three acts: first, the plotters' final preparations and the discovery of Fawkes with the gunpowder in London; second, the plotters' failed attempt to ferment rebellion in the Midlands; and third, the more composed government investigation trying to make sense of the plot, which flushed and lured evidence from those in the wings and in hiding – much of it embarrassing for the government. A chronology detailing the events in their proper order appears at the end of the book. It gives us the luxury of seeing events in the orderly fashion they rarely assumed for participants at the time.

I have avoided the use of footnotes and instead put references to documents alongside their use in the text. This is intended to stress the accessibility of the documents to all of us, not just to the community of scholars who deal in footnotes. Though the majority of domestic state papers are seen on microfilm at The National Archives, a great many of the other documents I use are still produced in the original to anyone with a reader's ticket who wishes to consult them. There is only one thing better than the high-quality document images in a book such as this to bring the voices of the players behind the plot to our ears – and that is to see the originals for ourselves.

... of his returne, as for these trompe...
wes founde upon him, the signification & ~~used~~ use of everie one
...time wolde be knowin, & quhat I have observit in thaim, the bea...
...ll show you, now laste, ye remember of the crewallie villanouse pa...
...at rayled upon me for the name of brittaine, if I remember ri...
...spake some thing of harvest & prophecied my destruction about ...
...me, ye maye thinke of this, for it is lyke to be the laboure of suche ...
...sperate fellowes as this is, if he ... the g...
...tours are to be first usi...
so god preserve your ...

Arendel house
Beere bayting h
Baynards

'A Muse of Fire'

THE THREE ACTS of the Gunpowder Plot are full of dramatic elements. The plotters were self-conscious performers, donning special clothes and props for their part as martyrs – scarves embroidered with exhortations and swords engraved with Christ's passion. There were also theatrical aspects to the plot: anonymous letters, prophecies and a suitably ironic moment when the plotters, making their final stand, were blown up with their own gunpowder. Drama was also important in shaping how people of the time viewed these events. The plotters and their contemporaries were the original audience of William Shakespeare's history plays: they could see played out in them the machinations of the court, the intrigues of succession, and the historical role of one of the eminent families who had, and still had, the power to make and unmake kings.

Plays could also be 'occasional', in the sense of dealing with specific events. Shakespeare's tragedy *Macbeth* – 'the Scottish Play' – was first performed in the months following the Gunpowder Plot, and its author could not resist articulating some of the malcontents' sentiments at the accession of the new Scots king to the English throne. In addition, what wordsmith could forbear to comment on the doctrine of equivocation – the poet's theology that allowed you to say two things at once? When we look at the plot's background in the light of the Jacobean theatre, we begin to appreciate it through the eyes and ears of Shakespeare's audience.

'Here, cousin, seize the crown': James I and VI, and the lessons of history

With the succession of James VI of Scotland to the English throne in 1603, the stage was set for intrigue and incident, for a fascinating *mélange* of major players and minor roles. As king, James might be expected to sit above the unfolding of the Gunpowder Plot, looking down in splendid detachment on the machinations below. In his own favourite form of drama, the court masque, however, he was more central and involved, enthroned on stage while the courtiers performed around him; James was very much one of the characters of the Plot and the players around him appear in a variety of guises, their chameleon-like roles often changing with circumstances or shifting to accommodate the audience. He was already an experienced survivor of plots and an expert at making political capital from their discovery; he was also a plotter himself, who had contemplated a military invasion of England before Elizabeth's death. Much of the air of conspiracy, the odd closeness of the plotters to the king and government, can be traced to the king's own plotting before 1603. As the investigation of the plot continued, it became evident just how close James and his ministers were to the plotters.

Early in his reign, James had restored to favour families who had supported and intrigued on behalf of his mother, Mary Queen of Scots, against Queen Elizabeth, rewarding their loyalty to his dynasty in adversity. Before Elizabeth's death, he had fostered links with the Earl of Essex as the strongest English advocate of his claim to succeed to the English throne, drawing back just far enough not to be implicated in the earl's ill-fated rebellion of 1601. The night before that rebellion saw a specially commissioned performance of Shakespeare's play *Richard II*, which seemed, at least in part, to justify the deposition of the reigning monarch. Those imprisoned and questioned after the failure of the Essex rebellion provide a reasonable initial cast list for the players behind the Gunpowder Plot: Lord Monteagle, Francis Tresham, Robert Catesby, John and Christopher Wright, and the Earl of Northumberland's brothers Charles and Jocelyn Percy were among those detained. Shakespeare and King James were able to talk their way out of it. The real lesson of *Richard II*, especially in the context of the plays that follow, is that the usurper has set a precedent which undermines his own position. He who lives by the plot will die by the plot. James was too committed a plotter to be deterred by this lesson, but years of plotting and counter-plotting in Scotland meant he was all too aware of the risks. He had engaged in shadowy secret correspondence with various groups in England before 1603, and conveyed words of comfort to English Catholics. Unfortunately for James, those who plotted on behalf of his mother had done so not merely out of loyalty to his family, but out of a desire to replace a Protestant king with a Catholic one. The motley assortment of malcontents who had rallied to

An imposing portrait of James I and VI by John de Critz the Younger. The new king of England had obvious potential allies in the Catholics who had suffered under Elizabeth.

Essex in 1601 remained predictably discontented into James's reign.

The English Catholics found themselves confronted by a monarch not only as convinced a Protestant as Elizabeth had been, but also one who wrote and spoke about theology and derided the 'superstitions' of Catholics more openly and more often. It was only natural that the new king should try and extend his patronage to – and be connected with – those who had suffered under Elizabeth. Yet it is still constantly striking how many of those involved in the treason designed to blow him up in November 1605 had been engaged before 1603 in an earlier treason, designed to assure his place on the throne. There was also a lingering question as to how broad and deep the support for the new foreign monarch was. Who could he really rely on among these former plotters, and who was simply waiting for the chance to replace him?

James's succession to the throne was a plot in itself, the product of an extraordinary secret correspondence with Queen Elizabeth's principal secretary of state, then Sir Robert Cecil; he was later rewarded by James with the earldom of Salisbury. Councillor and prospective monarch corresponded using code numbers to disguise their identity, involving a few trusted noblemen in a benign conspiracy behind the queen's back to ensure a smooth succession in the event of her death. James was still playfully using the code numbers of the secret correspondence in 1605. It formed a bond between him and his fellow erstwhile conspirators who were now the government. While James and his new councillors enjoyed playing at intrigue from comfortable positions of power, a whole host of shadowy figures, plotters, malcontents and place-hunters who had not gained what James had promised or hinted at while wooing interest groups south of the border came trailing in his wake, in search of belated reward or revenge. One of these was the man who had heard the verbal assurances given by the king to English Catholics and exaggerated them to emphasize his own importance, Thomas Percy.

Francis Bacon, lawyer, philosopher, poet and courtier, was also one of those who took a variety of routes on the rocky road to advancement. Bacon had been a dependant of the Earl of Essex, but was instrumental in his trial after the earl's rebellion in which so many of the plotters and their allies were involved. He also drew up 'A Declaration of the Practises and Treasons attempted and committed by Robert, late Earl of Essex'. Was this an act of unscrupulous betrayal or good judgement? Bacon's movement towards the now dominant Cecil was rapid. Cecil helped him with his already impressive debts and must have regarded Bacon as a clever man, better to have on your side than against you, but not entirely trustworthy. Having recommended himself by annoying Queen Elizabeth with his parliamentary speeches, Bacon held out hope of office under the new king. In a letter sent to the Earl of Northumberland in 1603, Bacon praised James's even-handed, if rather indiscriminate, bestowal of honours on his progress south. Bacon soon found himself a beneficiary, but, as he might have anticipated, it was hardly the individual recognition he sought; he was knighted in a batch of 300 others on 23 July. High office in keeping with his talents continued to evade him.

Many of James's councillors happily followed their monarch in plotting throughout these years. The consummate plotting councillor was Henry Howard, created Earl of Northampton in 1604. The involvement of the Howard family with the plotting and intrigue surrounding Mary Queen of Scots blighted Henry's political prospects under Elizabeth, despite his attempts to maintain court favour through flattering scholarly addresses. By 1595 he had hitched his star to the young favourite, the Earl of Essex, with whom he shared an elevated and self-congratulatory view of the importance of noble birth. Howard was too canny to involve himself in Essex's revolt in 1601, and immediately after it moved smoothly to the victorious Cecil faction at court. Sir Robert Cecil might have had reason to be suspicious of him, but Howard's well-established contact with James VI of Scotland was too valuable to overlook as James emerged as the likely successor to the English throne. In the secret coded correspondence with the king, Howard the 'long approved and trusty' was one of those plotting to ensure the smooth transfer of power after the death of Elizabeth. Scheming to ensure James's succession, Howard lost no time in plotting and elevating his own place in the future court. He warned James against other English courtiers, particularly Lord Cobham and Sir Walter Raleigh, both of whom were conveniently implicated in plots against the new king in 1603.

The 'Gunpowder Percys'

The family who had done most in Shakespeare's play to help Henry IV to King Richard's crown and who later reproached him for his ingratitude were the Percys, earls of Northumberland. The audience of Shakespeare's history plays could watch Percys rebelling and making and unmaking kings – generation after generation – every night, and might feel they had every right to expect rebellion from the latest incumbent. This was Henry, ninth Earl of Northumberland and head of one of England's great Catholic families, though he professed not to be a Catholic himself. Northumberland was a difficult man to fit into a straightforward role; there were too many facets to his character. One of these was an interest in military tactics. Ever since the first performance of *The First Part of Henry IV* around 1597, audiences had heard Northumberland's interests in artillery and ordnance articulated by his ancestor Harry Hotspur and would remember Falstaff's tremulous 'Zounds! I am afraid of this gunpowder Percy though he be dead.' The earl came from a background steeped in rebellion against the English crown and hostility towards the Scots, but he seemed to have been instrumental in the accession of England's new Scottish king and was restored to favour under him. Controversy has raged about the real extent of Northumberland's loyalty to King James and his complicity in the Gunpowder Plot through his cousin, Thomas Percy. Northumberland's pleas of innocence were not helped by the ambiguity of his language; his letters betray an astute nobleman biding his time, waiting to see what came of things. The earl also appeared in so many guises. Was he the real power behind the plot, or one of its intended victims – or, as he insisted himself, a man of private life who liked gardening and arcane scientific experiments and who had no interest in power? Sometimes it seemed he did not have sufficient power to control his own poor relation Thomas Percy.

Thomas Percy was one of those who did not undertake his master's prudent shift in religious belief, but who felt comparatively easy as a practising Catholic in the earl's service. Northumberland himself admitted he had followers set in their ways 'with oars in that boat'. It was obviously also an environment in which the occasional anti-Scots rant was perfectly acceptable. Nonetheless, Northumberland was a major figure in the secret correspondence with James in Scotland before the death of Queen Elizabeth. As his messenger, the earl selected Thomas Percy, and through him he sought toleration for English Catholics. In March 1603, as Queen Elizabeth lay dying, Northumberland was asked to join the council to oversee the transition, and there seems to have been a suggestion that the earl should act as protector of the realm while James made his way south from Scotland. In the event this was not required, but it may have sowed a seed of ambition in the earl and doubt in the minds of the council. Having suggested Northumberland for this role themselves, it is little wonder the authorities took seriously the suggestion that the Gunpowder Plotters might have expected the earl to act in the same capacity after the death of the king in the gunpowder explosion.

Northumberland continued fruitlessly to urge some form of toleration for Catholics once James was on the throne, and foreign ambassadors began to report that the earl was disillusioned with James and his Scottish entourage. Nonetheless, the earl gained office in keeping with his rank. He was sworn a member of the Privy Council in April 1603, and was appointed captain of the gentleman pensioners, the official royal bodyguard, in May, recruiting Thomas Percy.

In November 1603 Northumberland chose to recommend Thomas Percy to his king and remind James of Percy's past service in a letter about plots. The earl congratulated the king on his escape from the plots which surrounded his accession earlier in the year, themselves an indication that, though James is rightly said to have come to the throne almost unopposed, there were a great number of well-connected individuals who were malcontents or potential malcontents. Even those who worked most conscientiously to bring James to the throne could be opportunists as much as they were loyalists. There was much in the letter, as always with Northumberland, that could be read two ways. Recommending mercy as well as

NICHOLAS HILLIARD's portrait of Henry Percy, ninth Earl of Northumberland, shows him in contemplative, garden-loving pose. The Earl returned to this image in the wake of the plot to emphasize his lack of political ambition.

justice to the plotters of 1603, Northumberland reminded the king of the plot they were both involved in, as if to say 'while we're on the subject of plots, remember my servant Thomas Percy who was essential to the cloak-and-dagger negotiations for your succession, he'd like to see you again'. No wonder suspicion hung over Northumberland. His rhetoric about the plots of 1603 implicates himself in the anti-Scots language that Percy, and indeed Guy Fawkes himself, were all too fond of. The plot, he declared, 'carries with it the taint to all of us as are English'. The letter is heavily crossed through, as if Northumberland had struggled to find the right phrases. They are the careful words of a great man treading a fine line, rather than the joyous outpourings of a loyal subject.

18 November 1603†: Thomas Percy by owl-light

This ancient Mercury of mine my cousin Percy who could not before time look you in the face but by owl-light would be glad to see your majesty by daylight, poor men may have as great devotions as greater states … therefore to satisfy his desire and to excuse my absence if your majesty have not other service to command me, he most humbly kisseth your hands that will ever be found your majesty's most loyal and devoted servant N.

† calendared (SP 14/4/85)

There is some ambiguity about who the 'he' referred to here is – Northumberland talking of himself in the third person or Percy, acting for him or in his absence. Either way Northumberland seems to equate his loyalty with Percy's, five months before the latter took a vow to blow the king up. In retrospect, the king might well question how great that loyalty was. The letter was certainly seen as an unfortunate attempt at an introduction in the light of subsequent events. Percy's death before the authorities had a chance to cross-examine him has robbed us of valuable evidence of the speed and depth of his disillusionment. Though according to the evidence of Henry Garnet, Father Superior of the English Jesuit Province, suppressed by the king himself, many of the players behind the plot found the king 'odious'; of all the plotters Percy seemed most motivated by a personal dislike of James – perhaps because he knew him best. Percy's overly sanguine reporting of James's relentlessly ambiguous diplomatic language bore some responsibility for the 'disappointment' of Catholics in James's supposed broken promises of toleration, and Percy felt the king had deceived him. How much did Northumberland know of what was going on in the mind of his dangerous but indispensable cousin, and how much of what he knew would he tell the king? What were the feelings of Thomas Percy in November 1603, when Northumberland suggested to James that Percy would like to meet him openly after years as a secret go-between? Was he a man eager to accept his due reward now James was established on the throne, like so many others who emerged from the shadows on James's accession in the expectation of better times ahead? Or was he of the same mind as the Thomas Percy who only five months later was sitting in the Strand in London with Catesby, Thomas Wintour, Fawkes and John Wright devising the Gunpowder Plot? Perhaps the difference between these two versions of Percy is not, after all, that great, and Northumberland's 'misjudgement' of his loyalty is more understandable than it appeared to the authorities. The difference between the loyal Percy of the owl-light and the dangerous one of the daylight was not necessarily the result of a great shift in ideology, but a scale tipped by vanity and personal pique. He had helped put James in power, had boasted of his influence, but had not got what he wanted. Perhaps Percy's position was not in reality so far removed from Northumberland's own.

'Will the line stretch out to the crack of doom?'
Robert Catesby and Banquo's ghost

Robert Catesby's death alongside Thomas Percy at the siege of Holbeach robbed the plot of its most eloquent and motivated advocate. It also allowed him to be eclipsed in history by Guido Fawkes as the conspiracy's central figure. Had he survived to give evidence, we might burn Roberts instead of Guys on bonfire night, or even Robins, since this was how Catesby was known to his many friends, both among the plotters and their intended victims.

Robert Catesby was the son of Sir William Catesby of Lapworth, Warwickshire, and his wife, Anne, daughter of Sir Robert Throckmorton of Coughton – the very house that Sir Everard Digby rented from the Throckmortons as his base for the rebellion.

Sir

Theas offenders against your Ma: haue had all of them there tryalls (emongest the rest ~~these~~ two barrons) and are conuicted; I am gladde theas treasons haue bene discouered, since they tended to your safety, and by consequent to all our happynesses, for troubles in our cuntry may well pleas beggers, but will neuer content men that in=ioye good estates vnder you; And yett am I sorry for there persons, since it carryes with it a taint to all of vs as wee are Englische, for I could haue wished that my former iudgement ~~might haue had continuance as it ha~~ that neuer would haue lifted vp their had against you might haue had continuance as it had begining. I pray god your ma: may haue not more cause in examples of this nature to exercise thos attributes are giuen you ~~o~~ iustisse and mercy, bothe of them in ~~my~~ poore opinion ~~[illegible]~~ very well becomming you but most of all at this tyme: I will not say where I wische they should faule, least by naming perticular persons, my counsells might be construed rather to ~~[illegible]~~ be deliuered for ther sakes, then from the trew foundations of a iuste honest and faithfull counsellor. This ancient Mercury of myne my cousin Percy whoe could not before tyme looke you in the face but by owghlight would be gladde to see your Ma: by day light; poore men may haue as great deuotions as greater states, and all of them are to be cherished, therefore to satisfy his desiere and to excuse my absence if your ma haue not other seruis to command me, he most humbly kisseth your hands that will euer be found

your ma: most loyall and deuoted
seruant

H

Catesby was a descendant of the William Catesby who appeared as the 'cat' in the popular rhyme about Richard III: 'The cat, the rat and Lovell our dog, ruleth all England under a hog.' It is almost tempting in this context to see the Gunpowder Plot as a last Yorkist rebellion of disenfranchised country gentlemen who blamed the Tudors and their successors for planting and nurturing an alien religion in England and who sought a return to pre-Reformation English piety. There were plenty of plotters and priests in Catesby's circle with Yorkshire and Yorkist connections. Catesby's generation, the first audience of Shakespeare's history plays, was certainly expected to take a long view of history and to await the playing out of poetic justice over a period of centuries.

Many of the conspirators in the Midlands or their families were converted or confirmed in their faith by Edmund Campion, one of the Jesuits active in England. Catesby's father was one of Campion's hosts on his mission to England to re-establish Catholicism which ended in the latter's martyrdom in 1581. Certainly Robert Catesby believed that there was a hard core of Catholic families who would follow a strong leader, and that many others had adopted the new religion superficially in the hope of advancement rather than spiritual conviction – and would revert if the political climate changed.

Catesby seemed to be embarking on a conventional career, but the loss of his elder son and his wife in quick succession seems to have intensified his feelings of discontent with the world in general and his carelessness of his own safety. His part in the Essex rebellion led him to be wounded, imprisoned and fined. Together with his fellow Essex rebels and future Gunpowder Plotters John and Christopher Wright, Catesby was placed under arrest as a precautionary measure during the queen's last illness in 1603.

With the accession of King James, the unstable atmosphere prevailing since the Reformation, in which a change of regime and religion was only an assassin's bullet away, suddenly seemed to come to an end. While the excommunicate Queen Elizabeth could be dis-

NORTHUMBERLAND's letter to the king of *c.*18 November 1603 congratulated James on his escape from the plots of 1603, and then invited him to meet Thomas Percy – later a core Gunpowder plotter (see transcription p.20).

placed by Spanish invasion, there had been some prospect that a Catholic government was possible. Now a Protestant dynasty was ensconced with a Cecil dynasty to serve it – a relentless, unending succession similar to Macbeth's vision of Banquo's progeny in Shakespeare's play, first performed in the months following the discovery of the Gunpowder Plot. 'What,' cries the agonized Macbeth, 'will the line stretch out to the crack of doom?' (*Act IV.i*). You can hear a touch of Catesby's anguish in this cry, as it seemed to hold the prospect of the lot of Catholic families deteriorating forever.

'Faith, here's an equivocator': Father Henry Garnet and Catholic rebellion

Henry Garnet, Father Superior of the English Jesuit Province, was perhaps the most influential individual interrogated by the commissioners investigating the plot, and the one who caused them the most difficulty. He advanced two contradictory defences of his conduct in relation to the plot: one, that he was ignorant of it and two, that he had done all he could to prevent it. His evidence was difficult to evaluate and he infuriated his examiners – not least because they suspected, probably correctly, that he was cleverer than they were. His social ease with his questioners annoyed them, too, and popular rumour flourished about the priest who drank wine liberally, sang to the lute and inspired love in the women who protected him.

The authorities alternated the threat of torture with theological debate at which Garnet triumphed monotonously. Worse still, he interpreted the seal of the confessional so broadly that he felt able to conceal almost anything told to him in confidence from the authorities. Thanks to the doctrine of equivocation, which Garnet himself wrote about at length, he felt able to lie with calm religious conviction in a good cause. Though it cannot have been the first time the authorities were aware that a suspect was telling them less than the truth, Garnet's equivocations seem to have enraged them, threatening to undermine the whole basis of gathering and crediting evidence on which the investigation was based. Garnet's skilled equivocation achieved some celebrity, and made its way into the mouth of the porter in *Macbeth.*

> Faith, here's an equivocator, that could swear in both the scales against either scale; who committed treason enough for God's sake, yet could not equivocate to heaven. (*Act II.iii*)

Equivocation appears again in a serious context later in the play. The ambiguity of the witches' prophecy becomes 'the equivocation of the fiend that lies like truth' when Birnam Wood does, after all, come to Dunsinane. As always with Shakespeare, there is more than one way in which these lines can be read. Is Garnet's treason for God's sake? Will heaven see through the equivocator's lies or is he simply too devout to lie to heaven? Is equivocation devilish or is this simply a tyrant's view of a prophecy telling him the truth? Perhaps in their ability to say two things at once, the playwright and the priest had much in common.

A scholar and musician at Winchester College, Garnet did not make the expected transition to New College, Oxford, going instead to London. Here he contemplated a legal career and befriended Sir John Popham, later to supply much of the information on the Catholic underground in London as Lord Chief Justice and one of the investigators of the Gunpowder Plot. In 1575 Garnet travelled to Portugal and then Rome to join the Society of Jesus, becoming ordained around 1582. There was some doubt among his superiors as to whether the scholarly and contemplative Garnet was suited to the dangers and deceptions of the English Jesuit mission.

Garnet arrived in England at the time of the Babington Plot, which sought to place James's mother, Mary Queen of Scots, on the throne in place of her cousin Elizabeth. The ramifications of this made London too full of spies and suspicion to be safe. Garnet began to use and expand the network of Catholic country houses, later to shelter him in the wake of the Gunpowder Plot and the failed Midlands rebellion. After Garnet had been in England for less than a month, Father William Weston was captured by the authorities and Garnet found himself head of the English Jesuit Province.

Garnet was enthusiastic about Catholic prospects upon the accession of James I, writing on 16 April 1603: 'Great hope [there] is of toleration: and so general a consent of Catholics in the [king's] proclaiming [that] it seemeth God will work much.' Expectation quickly turned to disappointment and anger. Rumours of Catholic plots and conspiracies even reached Rome, and Garnet was instructed to do everything he could to prevent Catholics from resorting to violence. In June and July Garnet corresponded in Latin with the head of the Jesuits, detailing his attempts to restrain Catholic insurrection and gain time by persuading the plotters to seek papal guidance. Then on 25 July 1605, in confession, Garnet learned of a plot from the Jesuit Oswald Tesimond. In the late summer of 1605 he led a pilgrimage to Wales in a party including plotters, their families and friends; it passed through the plotters' houses where preparations for something momentous were evident. Was this a last attempt at dissuasion, an attempt to distance himself, a bestowal of blessing on the enterprise or a simple act of devotion unconnected with the plot?

Much of Garnet's evidence might be dismissed as unreliable, but it remains controversial and he himself has attracted vilification and vindication in equal measure. Despite Sir Edward Coke's attempt to turn the Gunpowder Plot into 'The Jesuit's Treason', there is little evidence to suggest that Garnet had anything to do with planning the plot – but he knew of it, was ineffectual in his attempts to stop it and did nothing to alert the authorities. It is perhaps a tribute to Garnet's symbolic importance as well as his evasions that so much evidence was taken from him and so much interpretation was placed on it. Whenever we are tempted to think of the plot in straightforward religious terms, it is always worth recalling the ambiguity of Garnet's role.

The evidence of witnesses to the plot is often ambiguous, not just because of the doctrine of equivocation, but because the language of the documents is theatrical and complex, the raw material of Shakespeare's plays. Do contemporary letters, notes and reports really tell us all we need to know about a character's convictions, enabling us to pigeonhole them on ideological grounds? Or do they show instead the dilemmas and confusions of characters gripped by more complex and ambiguous motivations? The voices of 400 years ago do speak through the documents, but to interpret their significance we need a fuller understanding of the plotters' world.

Act I: *Brimstone and Treason*

october to november 1605

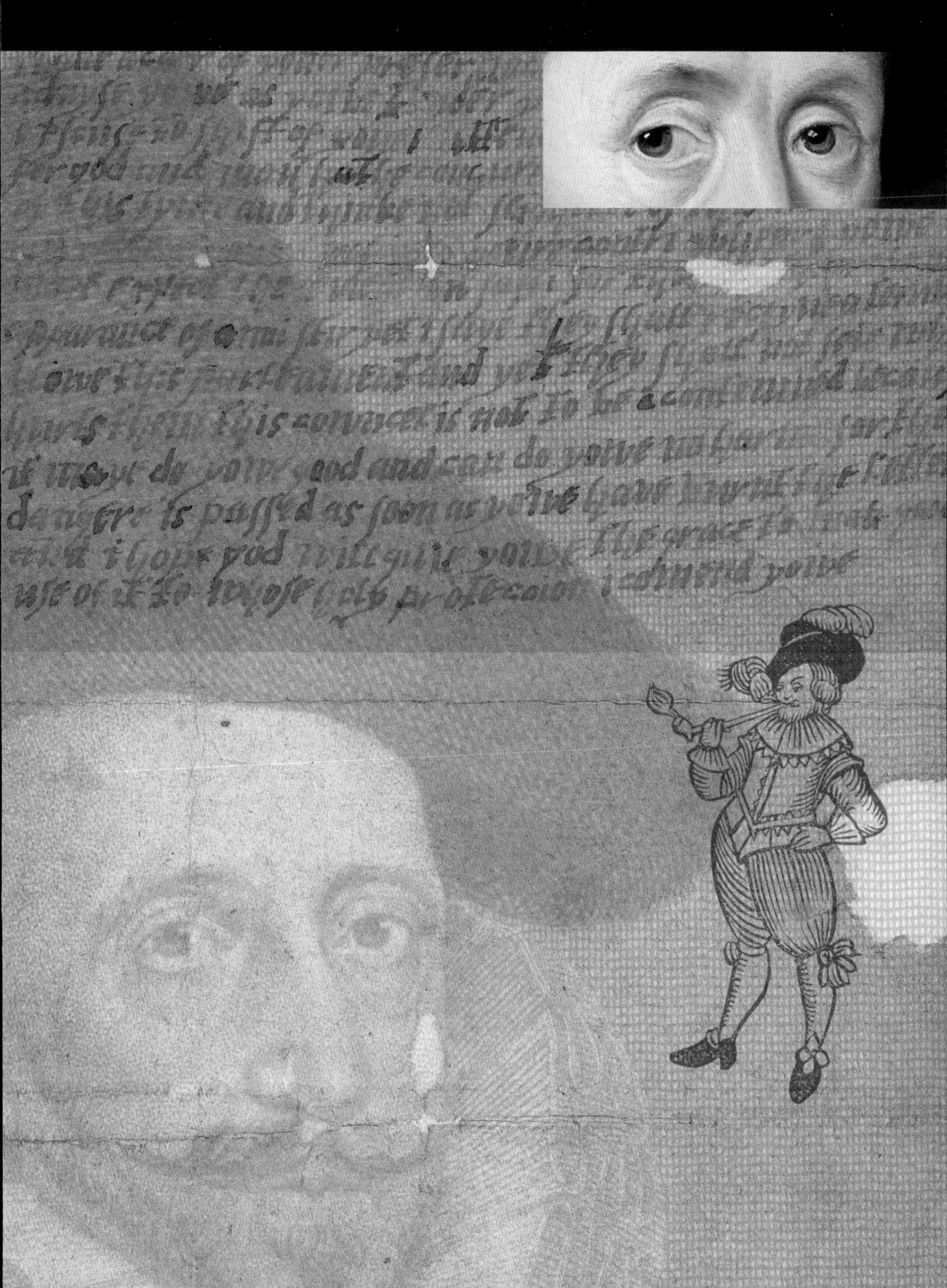

CAST LIST

James VI and I, King of England, Scotland and Ireland, 'odious to all sorts'

Henry Percy, Earl of Northumberland, captain of the king's bodyguard, 'The Wizard Earl'

Henry Howard, Earl of Northampton, Privy Councillor 'Conjuror of priests and devils'

Robert Cecil, Earl of Salisbury, Principal Secretary of State, 'The Little Beagle'

William Parker, Lord Monteagle, defender of Catholics in Parliament, recipient of 'The Monteagle Letter'

Anthony Maria Browne, Lord Montagu, nobleman, employer of Guy Fawkes

Sir John Popham, Lord Chief Justice, sometime friend of Henry Garnet

Sir Edward Coke, Attorney General, prosecutor and conspiracist

Sir Everard Digby, gentleman, of Stoke Dry, Rutland, and Gayhurst, Buckinghamshire, courtier

Francis Tresham, gentleman, of Rushton Hall, Northamptonshire, brother-in-law to Lord Monteagle

Robert Catesby, gentleman, of Ashby St Ledgers, Northamptonshire, and Lapworth, Warwickshire

Thomas Wintour, gentleman, soldier and scholar, secretary to Lord Monteagle

Thomas Percy, gentleman, member of the king's bodyguard, cousin to the Earl of Northumberland

Guido Fawkes, alias Guy Fawkes, alias John Johnson, gentleman, soldier

John Grant, gentleman, of Norbrooks, Warwickshire, brother-in-law of Thomas Wintour

Peers of the realm, gentlemen and ladies of the court
Servants, spies, placemen and players

Acting alone: Guy Fawkes and the Great Blow

We think of the Gunpowder Plot as a metropolitan drama, unravelling within the iconic walls and cellars of the nation's political heart. Though the Gunpowder Plot centred on London, however, many of the parties concerned showed a marked reluctance to go there. Luckily for us this led to a great deal of correspondence, since there was no other way of communicating at a distance, short of bonfires. We have letters from the king, hunting from his favourite base at Royston, to those councillors remaining in London, and others from plotters reluctant to leave the security of their network of family and friends in the country for the world of heretic place-hunters and informers in the capital. The plotters were almost as keen as the king himself on hunting, with its blend of fortune and skill. Both sides knew London as a place of political machination and back-stabbing where fortune and position could be won or lost in a moment, where people hunted other people and a misplaced letter could turn predator into prey.

In a letter written while hunting in October 1605, James apologized to Salisbury for his 'lack of matter', having little to say about state business, but confessed that, aside from his habitual financial embarrassments, 'I was never so void of care.' In the same letter to Salisbury, the Earl of Northampton's Catholicism is treated not as a threat but as a bit of a joke, an eccentricity that serves only to highlight his loyalty:

> ask of 3 how he thinks a priest can both make a god and eat a god and lodge both God and the Devil within him simul et semel. But I am sure that 3 loves so dearly his old 30 as he spares not to conjure both priests and devils for his master's service.

Here James jokingly continues to use his and Northampton's code numbers (30 and 3 respectively) from the secret correspondence before his accession – a shared intrigue of the past strengthening bonds in the present.

In the same month, October 1605, Northampton was involved in the preparations for the opening of Parliament and reported

Jesuit moves in the Low Countries to have the king excommunicated. He was also one of the councillors engaged in the king's great domestic struggle with his finances, and again conducted the reform of household expenses in secret as if it were a plot. Northampton may almost have wished the king was still writing to him in code in earnest; he repeatedly reminded the king to burn his letters, not trusting the grooms of the chamber who might read them and observing that 'letters are a prey which many hunt after'. Old habits die hard, and the new government still betrayed some of the fear and caution of plotters.

When he was not 'void of care', James was famously nervous of assassination attempts and plots. London, with its anonymous crowds, seemed a dangerous place. He preferred the feudal security of the hunt. Nonetheless, he seemed to have less cause to be nervous in England than in Scotland, where noblemen lived in proper fortified castles and thought nothing of kidnapping and imprisoning their king until their demands were met. In England his councillors lived in domestic security, in houses whose crenellations were just affectations of style. Only the landed Catholic families lived in true medieval fashion under real fear of siege, behind moats and drawbridges, their houses full of gothic features to provide hiding places for missionary priests, ever wary of the periodic punitive searches and confiscations of pursuivants. What was the real nature of their loyalty to the king? For James and those who relied on him, their existence was a constant conundrum. Were they really as passive and conservative as they seemed, or did they have the resources to break out and turn on their oppressor? James seemed to be continually in two minds about the Catholics, deriding their superstition but cultivating and advancing those such as Northampton who conformed outwardly.

While the king hunted at Royston under the watchful eye of Robert Catesby – who often shadowed the royal party from his house at Hillingdon in Middlesex – the plotters planned their own

JAMES I and VI by the circle of John de Critz (detail). The king made a favourable personal impression on his English subjects when he succeeded to the throne in 1603 – his reputation for ill looks and unpleasant habits came later.

Right trusty and welbeloved Cosen whereas ~~I~~ we
have receaved the company of Pencioners into
~~my~~ our grace and service, and have accordingly
admonished them what belonges to theyr duties
in theyr charges, because that some of them
were absent or owt of hearing ~~I would have~~
you particularly explane ~~my~~ our mind unto them.
And first and especially ~~I hold it fitt to have~~
th'oth of Supremacy be taken by every of them,
~~Then would I have~~ that you take particular Informacon
whether they are of meanes and ability to
maintaine themselfs in that sort as the place
requires: ~~Lastly I will have it expressly~~
forbidden that no man shall make sale or
trafique of his place for any consideracon.
~~And this being th'effect of my will and~~
~~pleasure in this affaire I bid you hartely~~
~~farewell~~ Given at Greenewich ~~this~~
day of May 1603 and ~~the~~ first
yeare of owr Reigne.

hunting party. Catesby and his companions conceived of a gathering at Dunchurch, Warwickshire, which would use the cover of a hunt to disguise a rebellious uprising; in the course of it James's elder daughter would be kidnapped from Coombe Abbey following the death of her father and brothers in the London explosion. The conspirators' notes at this time show an element of bravado rather than the fatalism that emerges from the official evidence reconstructing the plot after its failure. The time for action was near, and the plotters relished the occasion; the mood of their correspondence appears jauntier than James's coded notes or Northampton's restless desire to burn official letters.

Meanwhile, both the plotters directly concerned with the gunpowder end of the operation and their intended victims converged, with varying degrees of reluctance, on London. Suspicion of the city was endemic. Ben Jonson, the poet and playwright who had his own murky role as a player behind the plot, was well acquainted with the saying of John Hoskyns – whom he called his 'father' in literary style – that 'all those that came to London were either carrion or crows'. In Jonson's comedy *Volpone, or The Fox*, his theatrical response to the plot, the merchant Corvino – 'the crow' – is seen on stage along with characters named after other predatory birds and animals. As in the intricacies of the real plot, however, the roles of predator and prey change from scene to scene.

Jonson emerges from the events of the Gunpowder Plot as an ambiguous and shadowy figure. He presents a number of images of himself through his poems, plays and recollections: the former soldier and convivial but dangerous drinking companion who killed another poet in a duel; the meticulous classical playwright, critical of Shakespeare's lack of editing; and the comic dramatist celebrating the tricksters who thrive amid London's greed and duplicity. Yet simultaneously Jonson appeared to hesitate in the wings as the great drama of the plot took centre stage, seemingly determined to play as small and invisible a role as possible. In the summer of 1605 he

A letter from James to Henry Percy, Earl of Northumberland, 18 May 1603. The king commands his captain of the Gentlemen Pensioners to ensure 'first and especially that the oath of supremacy be taken by every one of them' (SP 14/1/86).

had been imprisoned, voluntarily, he claimed, in solidarity with his fellow playwrights, for a play called *Eastward Ho!* – a collaboration between Jonson, John Marston and George Chapman. The play, performed at Blackfriars by The Children of Her Majesty's Revels, satirized the king's liberality in bestowing knighthoods on his Scottish followers, and – worse still – mocked their foreign accents. The threat of mutilation as libellers hung over the three men, but in the event they were released unhurt. This could simply be an example of James's indulgence towards Jonson, already writing regularly for The King's Men, the king's own company of players, but it might also be that the authorities expected something in return.

Plans and Preparations

Much of what we know of the events leading up to the discovery of the Gunpowder Plot and the version of the story which is usually told is reconstructed from the examinations and declarations of the principal surviving plotters. Key amongst them were Thomas Wintour and Guy Fawkes, and additional information about the mind and motivation of Robert Catesby was supplied by Robert Keyes and Ambrose Rookwood. Whatever our view of this evidence, one thing about it is clear. It was written in the full knowledge of the failure of the plot and the near certainty of their execution, and tends to paint a rather fatalistic picture in which the chances of success seem absurdly remote. The whole attempt appears so flawed that even Catesby's powers of inspiration and magnetism seem insufficient to sustain it.

Documents written by the plotters at the time, however, are in a very different tone. It is true that they have been abandoned by Spain and the Protestant succession stands as an immovable barrier to the prospects and prosperity of them and their families, but their resolution to act alone has come as a relief. No more intrigue, diplomacy

THIS LIST of indicted popish recusants in London and Middlesex is dated 15 February 1604/5. It includes Gunpowder plotter Ambrose 'Roughwood' [Rookewood] and the writer and doctor Thomas Lodge, refused a licence to practice medicine by the College of Physicians because of his religion (SP 14/12/80).

The names of such Popish Recusants as were indicted at the Sessions holden for London and Midd the 15th of Februarie 1604

Midd.

Robert Gowen
Thomas Gowen
Roger Woddrington
Katherin Gowen
Arden Wasfere.
Thomas Hoord
Robert Hart.

William Wrench
Margaret his wife
Margaret Warde
Elizabeth Gee
An Daunce
William Hawkins
Oven and Hawley.

} apprehended in great St Batholmewes.

London

Richard Benson
Samuel Lane
Hughe Speake
Richard Hatton ar
John Web ar
John Moore ar
Frauncis Plowden ar
William Middleton ar
James Welford gen
Walter Waller gen
William Greene ar
John Web med
Ambrose Rougherwood ar
Henry Dorrell ar
John Povey gen
Roger Lawson ar
Raphe Lawson gen
Thomas Lodge D. of physick
Xpofer Askwithe gent.
Hugh Holland gen
Thomas Roper Salter
John Dabridgcourt. in prison
Frauncis Bowen, gent. in prison.

All theis indicted of Recusancie at the Sessions last 15. Feb. 1604.

Edward Norton prest
Alice Tempest
Frauncis Price
Simon Price
William Wymie
Katherine Jury
Phillis Wheeler
Thomas Proll

} apprehended in Grayes Jn Lane

In the Counter in Woodstrete

Thomas Penkavel
Peter Penkavel
John Penkavel
Thomas Giles

} theis weare taken last night at St Johns house

In the Counter

John Waterman } taken in Southwark.

View of the house formerly the residence of Guy Fawkes, at Lambeth.

An aquatint of 'Guy Fawkes's house' at Lambeth by nineteenth-century artist W. Read. In fact the house belonged to Robert Catesby and was used during the plot to store gunpowder under the supervision of Robert Keyes.

and disappointment – their fate is in their own hands. If not at ease in the wider society, the plotters are content in their own circle. The Catholicism that marks them among their own countrymen as something to be scorned or feared is among themselves a badge to be flaunted. They liked to show themselves as something apart from their fellow men. Thomas Wintour's reading matter was exotic and his clothes flamboyant; Ambrose Rookwood's flashy riding waistcoat, 'unfit for his degree', showed his pride in his horses, but also an unwillingness to be constrained by an uncongenial society's idea of what he should wear. Even Guido Fawkes's choice in rendering his Christian name was a challenge to the narrow isolation of Protestant England.

Anything outside their narrow circle was suspect. Catesby and his fellow conspirators seem in truth to have been singularly unimpressed by many of the forces that the authorities believed might be assisting their rebellion. They admired the Jesuits for their courage, but were impatient of the sophistications of their theology; they courted Spain as a source of patronage, but showed no surprise when it failed them; and they consistently maintained a genuine hostility towards 'foreign princes', among whom they counted the Scottish King James himself. The authorities who investigated the unravelling plot were convinced the conspirators were reliant on a 'great man' for patronage and support, but Catesby's contempt for the nobility was consistent and scathing. Even the famed network of Catholic women who sheltered the missionary priests and nurtured the faith in their households does not seem to have interested the conspirators, who excluded their wives and families as much as was possible. 'The people' as a whole seem to have barely entered the plotters' thoughts as a political force; it was assumed they would rally to whichever monarch under whichever protector Robert Catesby saw fit to proclaim, displaying the same docility with which they had accepted King James.

If the plotters were distrustful of all these groups, it is difficult to see where they expected their support to come from. The answer, presumably, was from other gentlemen like themselves, who had so far talked and done nothing but would follow their lead. Even within the ranks of the conspirators there were differing degrees of trust. Ambrose Rookwood, Sir Everard Digby and Francis Tresham seem not to have been in Catesby's confidence, but were rather seen as good-hearted, rich men who could be used and remain loyal.

Yet these players also had their own personalities and agendas. Tresham at least was as crafty and conscious of his own interests as Catesby himself, and this misjudgement of character by Catesby proved fatal to the 'project of the powder'. Digby, tall and handsome, naturally drew attention, and exploited his charisma successfully. He was appointed to household office at the court of Elizabeth I and was knighted by James at Belvoir Castle on 24 April 1603, during the new king's journey south to London. Four days afterwards, he appeared as a gentleman pensioner extraordinary at the Queen's funeral. Digby could have lived a comfortable life despite his religion, but the convert felt the plight of his fellow English Catholics keenly. Little more than two years after his knighthood, Robert Catesby was able to persuade his friend that he had a vital role to play in improving their lot by destroying James's government.

Subsequent documents suggest that persuading Digby of his own importance and of the rightness of Catesby's plot was not difficult.

Much of the detail of the plotters' preparations comes from Thomas Wintour's evidence given after his capture. As Catesby's lieutenant, he was the best informed of the surviving plotters who came into the hands of the authorities. Luckily the scholarly and rather witty Wintour also wrote some interesting notes to his fellow conspirators at the time, which give us an impression of their mood and motivations in constructing the plot without the distorting screen of hindsight.

As late as December 1603 Thomas Wintour was still doing his bit for the Catholic cause by fighting with the Spanish forces in Flanders. On 4 December he wrote a witty letter to his brother-in-law and later fellow plotter John Grant. His highly individual letter, emerging as it does from the heart of a bitter conflict, encompasses with dexterity the uncertainty of news, the accidental turns of history on such things as the weather, and the social rounds of Lord and Lady Monteagle.

4 December 1603: The fountain of news

Though I have been at the fountain of news, yet can I learn little to [*the*] *purpose, only a supply is expected by the Spaniards, some forty were taken in a little castle, which was surprised by our Lord Deputy, they confess that the rest are in some distress, having no store of victuals nor almost wood at all, and little artillery. Count Maurice is risen from Sitimgambes, some report with loss of 1500 men and most of his great ordnance, others say he was raised only by frost and hard weather, so tis uncertain whether tis true. Ostend is hardly pressed and likely to be won either by the Duke or by the Sea. This is all our news.*

Commend me to your mother and my sister, tell your sister Mary that my lady Monteagle is in the country, but I will shortly make a voyage thither on purpose, in her behalf.

So fare you well – this 4 of December your loving brother Tho: Wintour.

(SP 14/5/6)

Thomas Wintour's letter to John Grant, 4 December 1603, describes the bloody religious conflict in the Low Counties dispassionately and with wit. Some of the style of such letters survives in his confessions after the Plot's discovery.

6

17

Though I have bin at the fountaine of news, yett can I learne littell to pourpose, only a supply is expected by the Spaniards, some forty were taken in a littell castell, wch was surprised by our L: Deputy, they confess that the rest are In some distres: having no store of victualls nor almost wood at all, and littell artiler, Count Mauris is risen from Sitemgambes, some report wth losse of 1500 men and most of his great ordinance, others say he was raysed only by frost and hard weather, so is vncertaine whether is trw. Ostend is hardly pressed and likly to be won either by the Duck or the Sea. This is al our news. Commend me to your mother and my sister, tell your sister Mary that my lady Moundegue is in the cuntry, but I will shortly make a voyag thyther on pourpose, in her behalfe.

So far you well this 1 of December.

your loving brother

Th: Wentworth

The letter is written with some detachment by a man on the opposite side of 'our' lord Deputy. The Duke is the Archduke Albert, who led the Spanish force besieging Ostend, while Prince Maurice of Nassau was leading the Dutch revolt against Spain. It would be difficult for anyone unfamiliar with the campaign to follow which side is which. Cold weather and high seas seem as likely to affect the outcome as human action, but these God-driven forces do not favour one side or the other. The Spanish cause was theirs and not theirs, Catholic but foreign. As Spain moved towards peace with King James in 1604, it became clear that the real work for the Catholic cause would have to be done at home. Wintour was devout but had a practical soldier's view of the workings of providence in the affairs of men. They would have to act for themselves.

It was early in 1604, at the still-besieged Ostend, that Wintour met Guido Fawkes, during his latest attempt to establish whether practical support from Spain might still be expected. Fawkes had been a soldier in the Spanish army for many years and was largely unknown to the authorities in England, a great advantage to a plotter. He had also reported to the Spanish court the discontent of the English with their new foreign monarch. In further conversation at Dunkirk, Wintour told Fawkes that he and some friends were upon a resolution to 'do somewhat in England if the peace with Spain helped us not'. So Catesby, John Wright and Thomas Wintour disclosed the plot to Fawkes and Thomas Percy. They did so early in May 1604 at Catesby's lodging in the Strand in London, the five men having first received communion from Father John Gerard, the priest who had converted Digby to Catholicism. Fawkes, 'because his face was the most unknown', adopted the name John Johnson and assumed the role of Percy's servant.

As was revealed in Wintour's later declarations, corroborated by Fawkes and others, they originally planned to drive a mine under the Lords' chamber in Parliament. Progress was slow because of the thickness of the wall, the interruptions of their plans by the discontinuities of Parliament and the decision of the commissioners considering the abortive Union of England and Scotland to use Thomas Percy's chamber next to Parliament for their deliberations. No doubt Percy found this especially galling, given his dislike of the

Scots and his opposition to the proposed Union. At dinner with his patron, the Earl of Northumberland, at Syon House on the eve of the discovery of the plot, Percy could be seen waving a copy of the proposed articles of Union in disgust, remarking 'We have more in the North than you have here.' As delays mounted, they needed to recruit more conspirators to speed the work. Around this time Thomas Wintour wrote to his favourite correspondent John Grant to lure him closer into the plotters' circle.

26 January 1605†: Thomas Wintour, warrior monk

If I may with my sister's good leave, let me entreat you brother, to come over Saturday next to us at Chastleton, I can assure you of kind welcome and your acquaintance with my cousin Catesby will nothing report you, I could wish Doll here, but our life is monastical, without women.

† calendared (SP 14/12/39)

This letter to John Grant from Thomas Wintour reveals the plotters to be bound by more than the conspiracy itself. Ties of family, religion and culture made Wintour view them as 'monastical', withdrawn from the mainstream of English life.

'Doll' is Wintour's sister Dorothy, Grant's wife. Wintour jokes about their monastic life and their not entirely successful attempts to conceal their business from their families, but there is also a genuine religious edge to the letter. The plot was often referred to by its instigators in religious terms, an act in God's own cause; ascetic religious devotion has taken the form of a plot to blow up the government. The letter is conspiratorial, not just in its secrecy and what it does not say, but also in its Latin tags and references to Italian books. Our conversation and culture, it asserts, is different from that of our fellow Englishmen. Keeping women out of the way was obviously a preoccupation of the unmarried Wintour. He wrote to John Grant again in August requesting him to clear his house of co-conspirator Henry Morgan 'and his she-mate'. Yet not all the

A LETTER from Wintour of 31 August 1605 (below) betrays to John Grant a mistrust of all outsiders, especially women (SP 14/15/44). Writing from Antwerp to his brother Francis (right), William Tresham observes that the patronage of Spain could not be relied upon (see transcription p. 44).

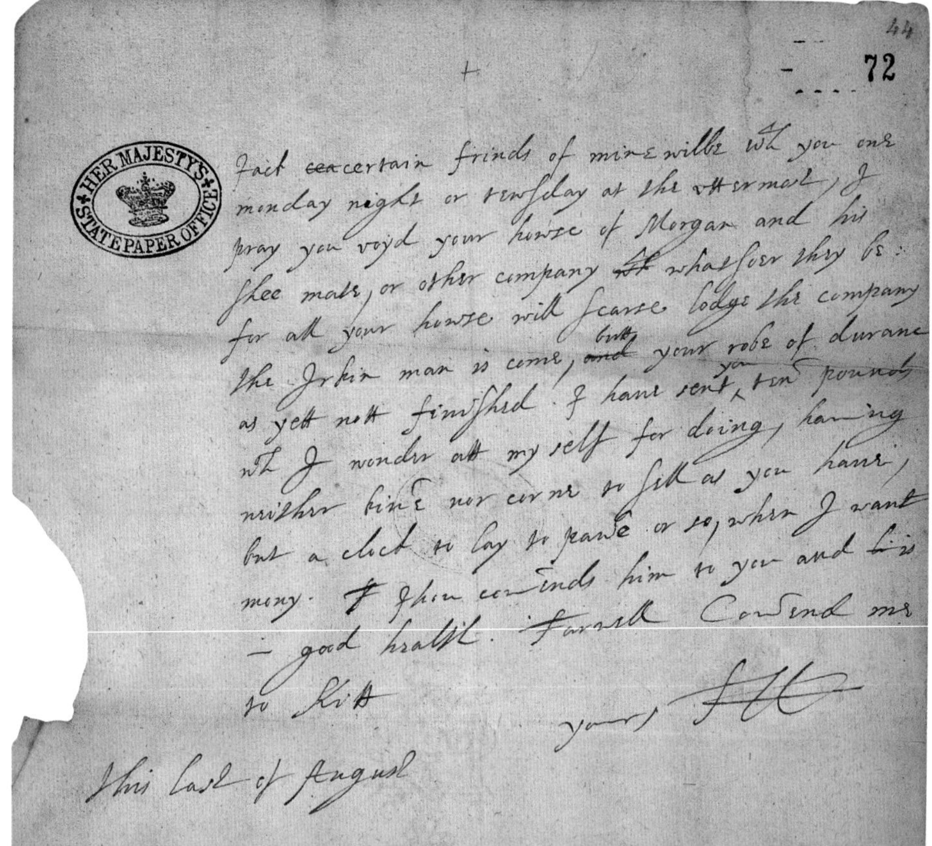

Jack certain frinds of mine wilbe wth you one monday night or tewsday at the uttermost, I pray you voyd your howse of Morgan and his shee mate, or other company whatsoever they be: for all your howse will scarce lodge the company. The Jerkin man is come, but your robe of durance as yett nott finished. I have sent you ten pounds wch I wonder att my self for doing, having neither kine nor corne to sell as you have, when I want but a cloke to lay to pawne or so, when I want [illegible] mony. I then commends him to you and his [illegible] good health. Farewell. Commend me to Kitt

yours,

This last of August

Sr. my longe staie of wrighting unto you: hath not bine, for forgetfullnes: haveing not anie newes worthie of sending: being verie sorie that my first, is noe better: I was in presence my selfe: therfore I thought good to acquainte you with the certaintie (as it is), the Enimie hath a place called Bergome opsome, which wee were to attempt upon with him 3000 men wee devided our forces into two partes; the one to geave one the one side of the towne, and wee the other. our men had made a Brige, which as they were entringe broake, now as our parte were entring, being but 300 English haveing the Vanne with Patavoes broke open the Portes, the Almaines which should have seconded us durst not so wee were prevented to; wee had 3 English Captaines ~~to our losse~~ Capt Dier. Capt Throgmorton. Capt John Blunte my Cap. being all hurte, of us English, were slaine 60 and 40 hurte which was more then all the reste. Sr you urged me much in youre last letter, for to be in a Spanish Companie one reason was, for to learne the language the other for sooner preferment: for the language, I acquowlege it and doe determine to bestowe some. 3 or 4 monthes in garison, under a Spaniard: for preferment there was never anie of our nation yt came to preferment under them. I have bine troubled wth a burning ague I thanke God I am now newlie recovered. I pray you send my monie to the same partie as the last was. for he is one, that heare can shew me a kindenes: thus ceasing to trouble you any further I end:

from Antwerpe the 26 September 1605

youre brother in all servis

William Tressam

plotters shared this view. Robert Wintour the family man did not feel the same detachment from fate as his bachelor brother, Catesby the widower or Thomas Percy, rumoured to be a bigamist.

Soon after the new recruits arrived, the vault beneath the chamber they had attempted to mine became available and the need for extra manpower disappeared. However, the group had grown and though Robert Wintour, John Grant and Christopher Wright were all trusty relations of the original conspirators, the risk of detection had increased.

Outside the plotters' circle at this stage – but not far outside it – was Francis Tresham. Heir of a leading Catholic family of Northamptonshire, his father's great wealth attracted punitive recusancy fines and stealthy negotiations to avoid them. Tresham's character and motivations, along with those of his brother-in-law Lord Monteagle, have given rise in retrospect to intense speculation. Like Thomas Wintour, Tresham had received intelligence of English Catholic disillusionment with Spain. On 26 September 1605 William Tresham wrote gloomily from Antwerp to his brother Francis about the career prospects of English captains in the army of Spain.

26 September 1605: William to Francis Tresham, disillusionment with Spain

For to be in a Spanish company one reason was for to learn the language, the other for sooner preferment for the language, I acknowledge it and do determine to bestow some 3 or 4 months in garrison under a Spaniard. For preferment there was never any of our nation came to preferment under them.

(SP 77/7 no. 235)

The letter from William Tresham is annotated 'This man is not at home.' Francis Tresham was always difficult to pin down, more so now, because Sir Thomas Tresham was dead and Francis had succeeded to his debts as well as to his massive estates. Unlike Thomas Wintour, Tresham did not believe the reponse to the abandonment of the English Catholics by Spain was to put his faith in Robert Catesby. On 18 February Francis Tresham had written to his father that 'in my cousin Catesby's promises there is little assurance'. Now, however, Catesby needed him. Suddenly he became someone who could raise large amounts of money quickly, an attractive prospect for Robert Catesby who had emptied his own pocket to fund the plot. Along with Ambrose Rookwood and Sir Everard Digby, Tresham was to be used for his wealth, but – unlike them – he was too wary of Catesby to fall under his spell. He would use his money to try and buy the plotters off rather than forward their enterprise.

On 12 October 1605, Thomas Wintour wrote to Robert Catesby pleading poverty, but in good spirits in the easy atmosphere of their Midlands stronghold:

> Though all you malefactors flock to London as birds in winter to a dunghill, yet do I, honest man, freely possess the sweet country air, and to say truth would fain be amongst you but cannot as yet get money to come up. I was at Ashby to have met you, but you were newly gone, my business and your uncertain stay made me hunt no further.

London was enemy territory, to be infiltrated but not dwelt in longer than necessary. When the decisive blow had been struck in Parliament, the next stage of the plot would take place in the relative safety of a network of Catholic households in the Midlands.

Though the details and evolution of Catesby's plan only emerged later, it seems always to have focussed on the Lords' chamber. There was a divine poetic justice in this for Catesby, for there the anti-Catholic legislation had been passed. From an ideological point of view the choice made perfect sense. Catesby was ready to attempt to save 'nobles that were Catholics' short of compromising the project: 'rather then the project should not take effect, if they were as dear to him as his own son … they should be also blown up.' The peers were 'atheists fools and cowards' almost by definition for taking part in the heretic government, though some sympathy was reserved for those who used their position to oppose anti-Catholic legislation in parliament. Looked at from the perspective of the plotters' social connections, things were far less clear-cut. For all Catesby's sweeping statements the Lords was well stocked with patrons, friends and family of the plotters, not least Catesby himself. Lord Monteagle had been a stout defender of the Catholic cause in Parliament; he had also been involved with Thomas Wintour and Guy Fawkes in their negotiations with Spain, owed money to Thomas Percy – and perhaps other plotters too – and was

The Thames at Westminster Stairs by Claude de Jongh (above) gives an impression of the higgledy-piggledy heart of London at the time of the plot.
The Monteagle Letter (right), delivered on 26 October 1605, prompted Lord Monteagle to confide in a group of Privy Councillors (transcription p. 48).

Francis Tresham's brother-in-law. Catesby himself seemed to be on close terms with Lord Montagu and Lord Mordaunt. When Keyes asked that Mordaunt might be warned against attending Parliament, Catesby promised that he would 'put a trick upon him, but would not for the chamber full of diamonds acquaint him with the secret for that he knew he could not keep it'. If they were bright enough to take Catesby's hint they would survive, otherwise they deserved to die. Some of the plotters unsurprisingly thought the hints might need supplementing.

Sir Everard Digby, not part of Catesby's original group of trusted plotters but brought in on account of his wealth, horses and connections, was one of those unhappy. His role was not in the gunpowder end of the operation, but in the subsequent rising. Sworn to secrecy, Digby questioned the proposed death of so many people, especially Catholic friends and allies in the Lords, but believed Catesby when he said he could trick their friends into staying away from the opening. 'Assure your selfe,' said Catesby, 'that such of the nobility as are worth the saving shall be preserved and yet know not of the matter.' This group, unknown to Digby, might be in single figures or even none at all.

'A Terrible Blow'

On 14 October 1605 came the fateful recruitment of Francis Tresham. Twelve days later, on 26 October, Lord Monteagle made the sudden decision to visit his house at Hoxton for the first time in several weeks, where he ordered supper to be prepared. A 'reasonable tall' stranger, his features fortuitously concealed by the twilight, left a letter with a servant of the house who happened to be outside. This in turn was passed to another servant who Monteagle asked to read it aloud while he ate – a request taken as evidence both of Monteagle's innocence and his complicity. The letter contained a thinly disguised warning of some explosive enterprise against the opening of Parliament. The letter was oddly worded and disguised by an artful illiteracy, but the meaning was clear enough.

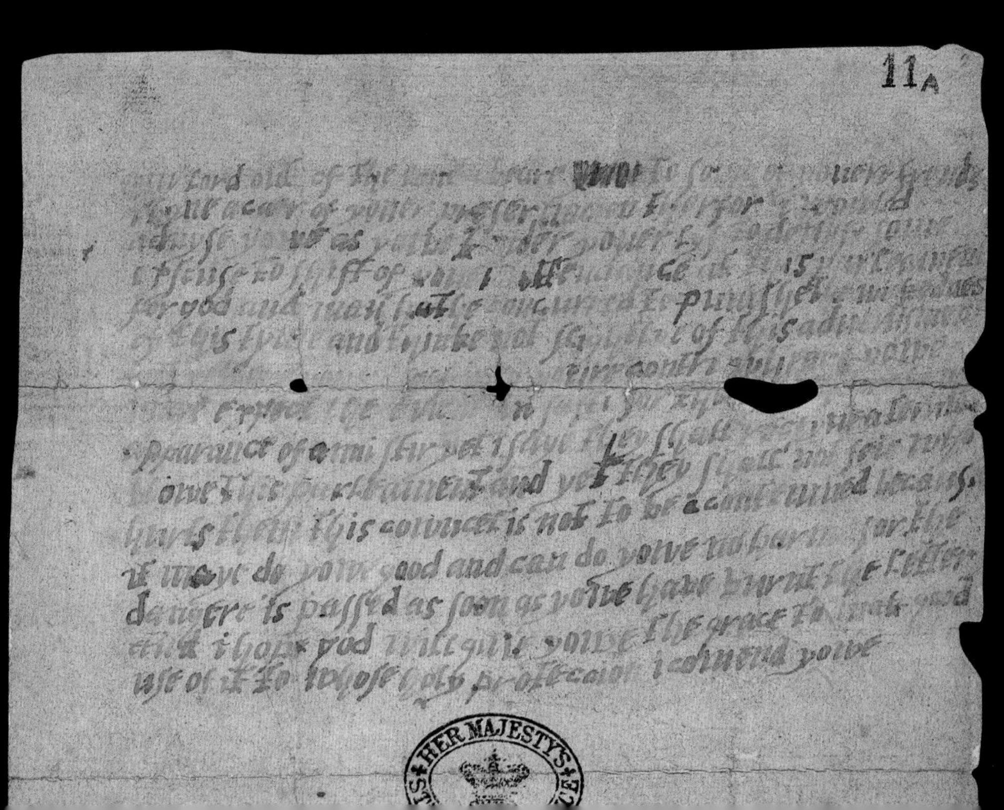

26 October 1605: Monteagle letter warning of the plot

My lord, out of the love I bear to some of your friends, I have a care of your preservation, therefore I would advise you as you tender your life to devise some excuse to shift your attendance at this parliament, for God and man hath concurred to punish the wickedness of this time, and think not slightly of this advertisement, but retire yourself into your country, where you may expect the event in safety, for though there be no appearance of any stir, yet I say they shall receive a terrible blow this parliament and yet they shall not see who hurts them, this counsel is not to be condemned because it may do you good and can do you no harm, for the danger is past as soon as you have burnt the letter and I hope God will give you the grace to make good use of it, to whose holy protection I commend you. (SP 14/216/2)

Luckily for us, Monteagle did not follow his instructions and burn the letter. Its authorship has provoked great debate. The plotters themselves identified the author of the warning letter as Francis Tresham, the lukewarm plotter who had offered Catesby money to forget the whole thing. Among those ingeniously supposed to have written the letter were Salisbury himself, keen to show off the efficiency of his intelligence network by inventing a plot for it to uncover. The heavily disguised and archly illiterate letter certainly suggests a writer known to Monteagle who wished to conceal his identity, though it has been suggested that Thomas Phelippes, Francis Walsingham's chief decipherer and the annotator of the 'Gallows Letter' which helped send James's mother Mary Queen of Scots to her death, might have been the man to concoct it. Perhaps only Francis Tresham knew his man well enough to know precisely what Monteagle would do with the information it contained – and was aware, too, that the warning would need to be disguised because Monteagle was too careful of his own new-found credit with the government *not* to tell them who had told him.

Tresham's moral and practical position in relation to the plot was rather like that of his brother-in-law Monteagle. He was of the plotters' circle and linked to previous plots, but he had dissociated himself from the Gunpowder Plot as soon as he heard of it and done all he could to prevent it except direct betrayal, which would have put him at the mercy of the plotters and the authorities. The letter was a lame compromise but it worked, and was as brave a thing to do as for Monteagle to risk revealing it. Tresham never got the recognition and protection of the authorities, who showed no great curiosity about the author of the letter. Perhaps, since it must have come from one close to the plot, it would risk giving the conspiracy a human face. Tresham seems never to have claimed authorship of the letter to try and gain favour with the authorities – about the only evidence against his having written it – but since Salisbury's object was to preserve Monteagle as the sole loyal figure, this is hardly surprising.

Monteagle took his letter to Whitehall, where he found some of the most prominent members of the Privy Council at supper. Salisbury's initial reaction to the letter seems to have been sceptical. In the official account of events, James, in his Old Testament wisdom as a Joseph or a Daniel, was shown the letter on return from his hunting at Royston; he immediately grasped its significance, to the admiration of his hitherto mystified councillors. This is not quite as incredible as it sounds; James's father, Lord Darnley, had been killed in a gunpowder explosion in suspicious circumstances in 1567, and the king was always sensitive to the possibilities of assassination.

The substance of the Monteagle letter was quickly passed on to the plotters. Thomas Wintour was, after all, well known in the Monteagle household: he had served Monteagle as a secretary for several years, and had actually attended the prorogation of Parliament on 3 October 1605 in Monteagle's entourage. Wintour gave the news to Catesby counselling discretion, if not emigration, but Catesby had another card up his sleeve. As Wintour later reported,

> He told me he would see further as yet and resolved to send Mr. Fawkes to try the uttermost, protesting if the part belonged to myself he would try the same adventure. On Wednesday Mr. Fawkes went and returned at night, of which we were very glad.

Fawkes was sent out in ignorance of the peril he was in, to see if anything was amiss, once more the 'unknown face' being most likely to escape detection. Fawkes later stated that he would have gone in any case, even if he had known of the letter.

Armed with their knowledge of the warning given to Monteagle and what he had done with it, Thomas Wintour and Catesby confronted Francis Tresham at Barnet on Friday 1 November. They accused him of betrayal; he denied it, trying again to deflect their purpose. We have a graphic surviving document which indicates Tresham's fear but also his sincerity in wanting to export the plotters and himself at this time: a licence granted to him to 'pass beyond the seas' for two years.

2 November 1605: Passport for Francis Tresham

A licence for Francis Tresham of Rushton in the county of Northampton Esq to travel beyond the seas with two servants, three horses or geldings and £50 in money with all other his necessaries and there to remain two years after his departure with provisions usual, dated the second of November, procured by Sir Thomas Lake. (SO 3/3)

Tresham never made his escape. Perhaps he was under too much pressure from the plotters who wanted him where they could see him. Perhaps he felt he must stay and do all he could to prevent the ruin which he felt would follow the discovery of the plot wherever he was.

Information about other plots was still landing on Salisbury's desk all the time, a reminder that the Monteagle letter was only one of a number of possible plots to be pursued. On 2 November, a letter partly in cipher about a possible assassination attempt landed on Salisbury's desk. Found in the street, it described the participants as the 'actors' and expressed a desire to see 'the tyrannous heretic [King James] confounded in his cruel pleasures'.

Rushton hall, Northamptonshire (above). When Francis Tresham inherited Rushton, he became a potential funder of Robert Catesby's schemes. As shown by the passport issued on 2 November 1605 (right), Tresham sought to use his money to persuade Catesby to abandon the plot, and then to leave England.

Tresham Licence ✓

A licence for ffrancis Tresham of Rushton in the County of Northampton Esq to travell beyonde the seas with two servants three horses or geldinge & fifty pounde in money wth all other his necessaries & there to remayne two yeares after his departure. wth provisions usuall. Dated the second of Novembr. procured by Sr Thomas Lake. — by the K.

A lre to the Lord Tresr of England to give order to John Taverner Surveior of his maties woode on this side Trent to cause the nomber of lxxx Tymber trees appoynted for the repairinge and fynishinge of the pales and lodge of the myddle parke at Hampton Courte to be felled within his maties mannor of Sonninge in the Counties of Oxford and Berks and from thence to be carried to Hampton Courte. Dated at Westm the second of November 1605. procured by Sr Tho. Lake. — pro R.

A lre to the Deputie of Ireland requiringe him to signifie to his maties Tresr or his other officers there and to the President of Mounster that the said President shall deteyne out of his rent for the ympost soe much as shall suffice for himself his retinue & the dyett of the Councell onely and yf those rents will not serve then to supply yt out of the revenues of that Province but the rest of the garrisons to be payd by the Tresr as money shall come to his handes. Dated and procured as above. — pro R.

A lre to the Tresr at warres of the Realme of Ireland to pay to Edward Dodington one of the Captaynes who hath a pencon of iiijs Irish harpes by the day payable in Ireland all such arrerages as are due unto him uppon his said pencon since the tyme that by licence from the Lieutenant of that Kingdome he hath bene at the bath for cure of his woundes receaved in service or elsewhere in this Realme and soe from thence forth to pay unto him his said pencon here within this Realme for soe longe tyme as yt shall appeare to his maties said Tresr that the said Dodington is licenced by the Lieut or Deputie of Ireland to be absent in regard of his health. Dated & procured as above. — by the K.

Tirell Han[illegible] ✓

Broome & Licence ✓

Cave Licence ✓

Treasr & a Warra[illegible] ✓

Sr Charles Cornewal[illegible] Warra[illegible] ✓

On the evening of 3 November, Thomas Wintour and Robert Catesby met Thomas Percy, who had recently arrived from the north 'on the King's own especial service'. Percy stiffened their resolve and offered to go to Syon House to dine with the Earl of Northumberland to try and gauge the level of knowledge of the plot. This would seem to be another example of plotter bravado despite the suspicion of possible discovery. Percy appeared confident that he could go to dinner with a Privy Councillor on the eve of an explosion designed to destroy Parliament and manipulate the conversation to discover what the authorities knew of the plot without giving himself away. After the dinner, he was able to reassure the others that there was no sign of the plot having been discovered. So Fawkes took up his station in the vault, with a slow match and a watch, sent to him by Percy via Robert Keyes 'because he should know how the time went away'.

Meanwhile the Privy Council was treading carefully. To allow the plot to ripen, nothing further was done until 4 November. James hoped that, as the plan progressed, not merely those who were involved in its mechanics, but also those in power who were supporting them would be revealed. An initial tour by the Earl of Suffolk – responsible as Lord Chamberlain for preparations for the new Parliament – accompanied by Monteagle, provided the authorities with all the evidence they could have hoped for. They found Fawkes overseeing a large quantity of firewood in a vault rented by his master, Thomas Percy. Monteagle made a few pointed remarks to Suffolk as they returned, about being previously unaware of Percy, a Catholic, renting a cellar in Westminster. Fawkes was arrested and the gunpowder discovered.

At about 5 am on Tuesday 5 November, Christopher Wright came to Thomas Wintour with news of the discovery of the plot. Wintour, as he later confessed, rather in the manner of one of his witty letters, walked coolly to the court and then to the Parliament

THIS PASS, dated 25 October 1605, required local officials' aid for Thomas Percy 'to make speedy repair to the Court about his Majesty's special service'. Percy was returning from the northern estates of Northumberland, his patron and cousin – thought by some to be the 'great man' behind the plot (SP 14/15/106).

Robert Delavale knight and Edward
Grey Esquire, Comissioners for his Majestie
in the Northe

Forasmuch as this gent the bearer hereof Thomas
Percie Esquire is to make his spedie repaire by post
to the Court about his Mats speciall service
These are therfore to will and require, and in his
Mats name straitlie to charge & commaund you and
every of you to see him furnished from tyme to tyme
and place to place with three able & sufficient post
horsses and a guyde accordinglie at prices ordinarie
and accustomed. Whereof faile you not as you
and every of you will answer the contrarie at yo[ur]
perills. Given at Seaton Delavale
xxv° Octob. 1605

Ro: deLavale
Edward Grey

To all and singuler the keepers of his
Mats posts, Justices, Maiors, Sheriffes,
Bailiffes, Constables, Headburghes and
to all other his Mats officers and subiects
to whom these shalbe shewen, and to every
of them

house, but found both heavily guarded and the discovery of the plot being discussed. Wintour rode off in pursuit of Catesby and Percy who had left London the previous evening. The authorities only really began to suspect him the next day. Wintour rode to his brother's house at Huddington and from there to Catesby's house at Ashby. Here he received a message to meet Catesby in the fields away from the house and telling him the news he already knew: 'Mr Fawkes is taken and the whole plot discovered.'

With the discovery of the plot came an explosion of official documents. The secretive letters of the plotters and the shadowy notes from Salisbury's more or less unreliable informers give way to the bombardment of an official investigation, involving many of the principal officers of state and lasting eight months. For the first two months, the investigation of the plot seemed to absorb almost all the resources of government to the exclusion of all other business.

While Salisbury composed the official version of events, the court newsmonger John Chamberlain wrote to Dudley Carleton enclosing a copy of the Monteagle letter and reporting the now familiar celebrations which had greeted the discovery of the plot. 'On Tuesday [5 November] at night we had great ringing and as great store of bonfires as I ever I think was seen.' Carleton was a diplomat whose correspondence with Chamberlain in London gives a valuable insight into the rumour and gossip of Jacobean court life. However, the Gunpowder Plot turned Carleton from a detached, ironic observer of events to one of the figures at the centre of the greatest sensation of the reign. For weeks his career and future prospects hung in the balance, due to his connections with the lease of Thomas Percy's house and of the vault below Parliament.

Guy Fawkes in the vault below the House of Lords – complete with dark beard, lantern and barrels of gunpowder – is the abiding image of the plot and the focus of today's 5 November celebrations. Fawkes's identity was unclear for some time; the authorities knew

THE INITIAL examination of 'John Johnson' took place on 5 November 1605. Fawkes's wit and stubbornness under questioning both impressed and frustrated his examiners, and his replies were more anti-Scottish than anti-Protestant (see transcription p.57).

6

The Confession of John Johnson servant to Thomas Percy esquire, one of his Ma^{tes} pensioners, taken this Tuesdaye the fifth of November 1605 before the Lord chief Justice of England, and Sr Edward Coke knight, his Ma^{ts} Attorney generall.

15

A. Being demaunded when he went beyond the Seas, and if he did, to what parte he went; Answereth that he went beyond the Seas about Easter last, and toke shipping at Dover, but remembreth not in what Shippe he went, and from thence to Callice, and from Callice he went to St Omers, and was in the colledge there, and from thence did goe to Bruxels, and staid there about three weeke, and from thence went to Spinolaes campe in Flaunders, and was there about three week, and receyved no paie there, and in his waie went to Dowa, to the colledge there, and from thence returned to Bruxells, and remayned there about a Monthe, and sawe Sr Wm Stanley, Hughe Owen, Hugon Grentwaye, and divers other Englishmen, And from thence he went of Pilgrimage to the Ladye of Mountague in Brabant, where he was twise on Pilgrimage all alone, And confesseth that about the endinge of August, or the beginning of September, he returned by Callice, and so to Dover, and from thence he came to an Inne without Algate, hard by a Taverne, and the next daie he came to the lodging neere the upper house of Parliament.

John Johnson

[Margin notes:] Easter last. / St Omers / Bruzells / Spinolaes campe / Dowa / Sr Willm Stanley, Hughe Owen, Greneway, Hugon / pilgrimage / September

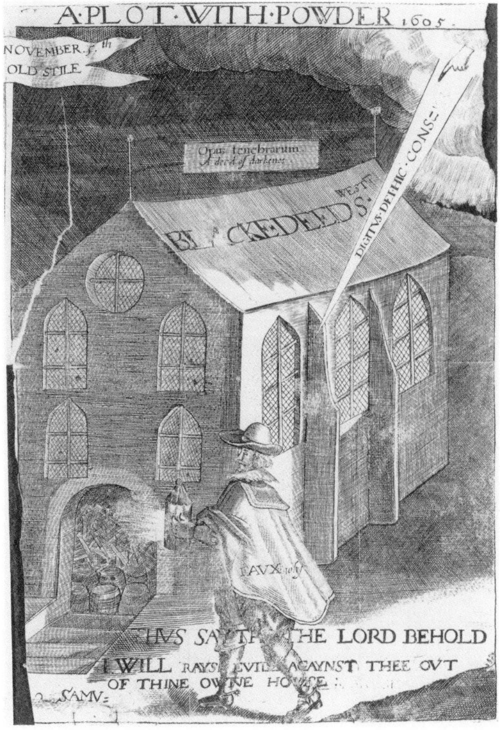

An engraving of 1603, 'A Plot with Powder' shows Fawkes as the central player in the plot. He was a genuine lone figure among the conspirators, removed from the ties of blood and patronage that bound many of the others.

him only by the alias he gave, John Johnson, and for a long week after the discovery of the plot he was questioned alone in the Tower of London, the authorities' only direct source of information. Documents show Fawkes's humanity, steadfastness and lack of repentance, making him a difficult figure to hate but also difficult to defend.

'Roman Resolution'

The examinations of 'John Johnson', though largely formulaic, give a clear indication of the character of the man. The wit and style of his replies, his stubbornness and contempt for his examiners and his distrust of foreigners are all consistent. His examiners wrote grudgingly of his fortitude, his 'Roman' resolution. Confronted with a barrage of questions, he refused to implicate his colleagues, apart from Percy, whose identity was part of Fawkes's own cover and would be clear to anyone who investigated the ownership of the vault. Fawkes admitted having recently travelled to Flanders, but when pressed for a reason the Spanish soldier mocked his examiners, declaring that he had set out 'to see the country and to pass away the time'. When he did speak plainly, it was to dispraise the Scots (an attitude evident when he had predicted English discontent with King James's accession in reports to the Spanish crown in 1603), to complain of the foolishness of the warning given to Monteagle and to express incredulity that he should even be asked to betray the other plotters.

5 November 1605: Initial examination of 'John Johnson'

C. And confesseth that when the king had come to the parliament house this present day, and the upper house had been sitting, he meant to have fired the match and have fled for his own safety before the Powder had taken fire, And confesseth that if he had not been apprehended this last night, he had blown up the upper house, when the King, Lords, Bishops and others had been there.

E. And being demanded if his purpose had taken effect, what would have been done with the Queen's Majesty and her royal issue, saith that if they had been there he would not have helped them.

F. And being demanded if the king and his royal issue had been all taken away whom would have been published or elected king, Saith Percy never entered into that consultation.

G. And being demanded when the king, his royal issue, the Nobles, Bishops, Judges, and of the principal of the Commons, were all destroyed what government would have been, Answereth we were not grown to any determination therein, and being but a few of them they could not enter into such conversation, but that the people of themselves would decide a head.

K. And confesseth that when this act had been done they meant to have satisfied the Catholics that it was done for restitution of religion, And would have drawn others by publishing that it was done to prevent the Union that was sought to be published at this parliament. (SP 14/216/6)

There were hints here of a wider conspiracy, though as yet the authorities had no firm evidence of it. No one could quite believe that the plotters had intended to sweep away the entire government without the support of powerful forces or any clear idea of the

Note Englishe souldiors cam against the beginning of ye plmt if it had not bene proroged

This treason was plotted before the end of the last cessyon of parliament.

the last cessyon beganne the 19 day of marche and continued untill the 7 of July ano 2 Jacobi Regis / ano 1o Jacobi 1604 and proroged untill the 7 of febr: and from thence untill the of october and from thence untill the 5 of Nov: 1605:

John Johnson confesseth that this treason hath bene plotted a yere and a halfe past which was before the Ende of the last cessyon. and the house was hyred by mr Thoms percy a yere and a halfe past

And because it tooke not then effect. it is to be obserbed that Johnson confesseth that about christmas last powder was provided and conveyed into the celler under the upper house of plmt which evidently was against the 7 of february to which tyme the plmt was proroged but the plmt then being further proroged untill october. Then he goeth over sea about Easter etc and returneth in september and provideth more powder and stones against october, the plmt then being further proroged on the 4 day at the night he had provided touchwood and a match which he had about him, and hearing them that cam to apprehend him cast it into the water

this must be 5 or 6 Nov. The 1st exam is in the name of John Johnson

obserbe the Englishe souldiors comming over etc against the day in october to which the plmt was proroged. and note by whose procurement they cam over etc.

the effect of mr Banx lre
fast and pray that the purpose may come to passe and then
Stream shall be turned frenche

A lre offered to Griffith

Rokewood / Sibords /
Winter

tabnall

The Englishmen
[illegible] against the beginning of
the plmt if it had
ben proroged

Note percy did find the key of the celler
and made

regime that was to come next. The man to find a conspiracy, even where none existed, was Sir Edward Coke, the Attorney General, who searched assiduously for a wider conspiracy behind the plot and greater men than the central plotters themselves to bring to trial. Sometimes in his zeal he exceeded the remit of investigation set by the king and Salisbury, and the results could be embarrassing to the government as well as enlightening. We have Coke's initial thoughts on the early examinations of 'Johnson' entitled 'my notes' in Coke's hand. Surprisingly to modern eyes, Coke was keen to pick up references to prophecy and astrology relating to the plot, something perhaps to explain the confidence of a group with such apparently narrow support. 'Johnson' was carrying a letter addressed to 'Mr Fawkes' (an alias, the prisoner explained), which contained the following riddle: 'fast and pray that the purpose may come to pass and that Tottenham shall be turned French'.

The fulfilment of so great a change as Tottenham turning French, which Coke interpreted as referring to a return to Catholicism in England, showed the Catholics falling back on prophecy where the practical help of Spain had failed them. To make the prophecy come true needed more than a few gentlemen plotters. In Coke's mind a 'great man' was indispensable to such an enterprise and he already had some names handy, among them the unlikely figure of Sir Walter Raleigh, already imprisoned in the Tower. In their quest for information about the whereabouts of the plotters, the authorities turned to Simon Forman, astrologer and physician. Though finding out the location of lost and sought-after people and objects was a standard part of Forman's trade, it is probable that his knowledge of the lives of his patients rather than his powers of divination was the real reason why Forman was consulted. He had Catholic connections; the patients who consulted him most frequently and confidentially were the wives of London Catholics who came to him, if we believe his diary, for his particular, unethical brand of fertility treatment.

Edward Coke, the Attorney General, made notes on the initial interrogations of 'John Johnson'. He paid keen attention to the prophecy found in the letter Fawkes was carrying: 'fast and pray that the purpose may come to pass and that Tottenham shall be turned French' (SP 14/16/7).

James, too, was fascinated by prophecies as well by the plotters and their motives. In a letter framing the questions to be used in the interrogation of 'John Johnson' and authorizing his torture, James linked him to the malcontents who had unearthed prophecies to oppose the creation of 'Great Britain'. In this he was at one with Fawkes, who in his examinations thought their opposition to the Union would be enough to make their Catholic government popular with non-Catholics.

James did not recognize but half expected to know Fawkes as he knew Thomas Percy, not just because of his plotting past, but also because of the small world of Jacobean court life. Though Fawkes posed as a servant, James suspected from his conversation and experience that he was no such thing. His social rank betrayed him as much as his unlikely alias. The king saw a class of man familiar to him and vital to the smooth running of the state. Thomas Wintour as secretary to Lord Monteagle and Fawkes as a member of Lord Montagu's household had the entrée to social events close to the king. One of Fawkes's pieces of evidence that never appeared in the official version of events was that he had been at a wedding attended by the king earlier in the year; even the demon outsider was not that far outside the charmed circle of the court. In setting out the questions he wanted Fawkes to answer, the king shows himself not only personally involved in his interrogation and torture, but also oddly similar to the suspect, ridiculing his Catholic superstitions and religious artefacts ('trumpery wares') while brooding on prophecies himself.

6 November 1605: James I's personal interest in the interrogation of Fawkes

The examinate would now be made to answer to formal interrogators:
As what he is (for I can never yet hear of any man that knows him)?
Where was he born?
What were his parents' names?

A letter from King James authorizing the torture of 'Johnson' (Fawkes) on 6 November 1605. Alert to plots, the king seemed to suspect early on that Fawkes was not Thomas Percy's servant as he claimed.

quhair upon it shoulde seeme that he hath bene ~~recomended~~ recomendit by
some personnis to his maisters service only for this use, quhairin only he
hath servid him, & thairfore he wolde also ~~and~~ be asked in quhat company & ship
he went out of englande, & the porte he shipped at, & the lyke questions
wolde be asked anent the forme of his returne, as for these trumperie
wares founde upon him, the signification & ~~and~~ use of everie one of
thaime wolde be knowin, & quhat I have observid in thaim, the bearare
will show you, now laste, ye remember of the crewallie villanouse pasquil
that rayled upon me for the name of brittaine, if I remember richt
it spake some thing of harvest & prophecied my destruction about that
tyme, ye maye thinke of this, for it is lyke to be the laboure of suche a
desperate fellow as this is, if he will not other wayes confesse, the gentler
tortours are to be first usid unto him, & sic per gradus ad ima tenditur,
& so god speede youre goode worke.

James R.

What age is he of?
Where hath he lived?
How he hath lived and by what trade of life?
How he received those wounds on his breast?
If he was ever in service with any other before Percy, and what they were, and how long?
How came he in Percy's service, by what means and at what time?
What time was this house hired by his master?
And how soon after the possessing of it did he begin his devilish preparations?
When and where learned he to speak French?
What gentlewoman's letter it was that was found upon him?
And wherefore doth she give him another name in it than he gives to himself?
If he was ever a papist, and if so who brought him up in it?
If otherwise, how was he converted, where, when, and by whom?
... *As for these trumpery wares found upon him, the signification and use of every one of them would be known. And what I have observed in them the bearer will show you. No last, ye remember of the cruelly villainous pasquil that railed upon me for the name of Britain. If I remember right, it spake something of harvest and prophesied my destruction about that time. Ye may think of this for it is like to be the labour of such a desperate fellow as this is.*
If he will not otherwise confess, the gentler tortures are to be first used unto him, et sic per gradus ad ima tenditur [and so by degrees until the ultimate is reached]. *And so God speed your good work. James R.*

(SP 14/216/17)

Some of these questions are straightforward; others seem more remarkable. James's idea that Fawkes might be a priest, for example, does not exactly chime in with the popular image of him. Many of the questions, whether remarkable or not, would prompt uncomfortable answers. Fawkes's experience overseas and language skills came as a result of his service in the Spanish forces in Flanders, service which James himself had come to sanction as part of the treaty

DRAFT proclamation for the apprehension of Thomas Percy, 5 November 1605. The Earl of Salisbury's draft shows signs of being hurried and revised, but drew on accurate information about Percy, well-known in court circles (SP 14/16/8).

a Jesuit ~~[illegible]~~ or ~~Tesmond~~ ~~[illegible]~~ Greenway a gentle
man persuaded that he was so disposed. to have
been privy to one of the most horrible treasons
that ever was contrived that is to have blown up
the king his noble ~~[illegible]~~ [illegible] would have been with
the upper house of the Parliament attended with
the [illegible] [illegible] all the nobility and the
commons with gunpowder the chamber where
they should be assembled, [illegible] is [illegible]
[illegible] [illegible] [illegible] all
[illegible] [illegible] subjects [illegible] to
[illegible] [illegible] doubt not but they will
[illegible] [illegible] [illegible] [illegible] all [illegible]
person for the said Greenway [illegible]
[illegible] especially to [illegible]
by all possible means [illegible]
[illegible] [illegible] the rest of the conspirators
[illegible] The said Greenway is a tall
man well disposed [illegible]
with a great broad beard a good face the
colour of his beard and head mingled with white
hairs but the head more white than the beard
and stoopeth somewhat in the shoulders well
coloured in the face long footed small legged
Given at our Palace of Westminster the [illegible] day
of November 1605 — the third year of our
reign of Great Britain

time aboue limitted execute the same, that they do prosecute their offence therein as in case of contempt by all such wayes and meanes, as in like case is usuall.

Giuen at our Honour of Hampton Court the 27. day of September, in the third yeere of our Reigne of Great Britaine, France and Ireland. Anno Dom. 1605.

¶ A Proclamation for the search and apprehension of Thomas Percy.

WHereas one Thomas Percy a Gentleman Pensioner to his Maiestie, is discouered to haue bene priuie to one of the most horrible Treasons that euer was contriued, that is, to haue blowen vp this day, while his Maiestie should haue bene in the vpper House of the Parliament, attended with the Queene, the Prince, all his Nobilitie & the Commons, with Gun-powder (for which purpose a great quantitie of Powder was conueyed into a Vault vnder the said Chamber, which is this morning there found) the Chamber where they should bee assembled, which Percy is sithens fled: These are to will and command

mand all our Officers and louing Subiects whatsoeuer, to that which we doubt not but they will willingly performe a[c]ding to the former experience we haue had of their loue and z[eale] toward vs, That is, to make all diligent search for the said Pe[rcy] and him to apprehend by all possible meanes, especially to k[eep] him aliue, to the end the rest of the Conspirators may be disc[oue]red. The said Percy is a tall man, with a great broad beard, a g[ood] face, the colour of his beard and head mingled with white hai[res] but the head more white then the beard, he stoupeth some whe[at in] the shoulders, well coloured in the face, long footed, small legg[ed].

Giuen at our Pallace of Westminster, the fift day of Nouemb[er in] the third yeere of our Reigne of Great Britaine.

Anno Dom. 1605.

¶ A Proclamation denouncing Thomas Percy and other his adherents to be Traitors.

WHereas Thomas Percy Gentleman, and son[...]

with Spain in 1604. The gentlewoman whose letter Fawkes carried was Eliza Vaux, a member of one of those Catholic families James had negotiated openly and amicably with over fines for recusancy.

Thomas Percy, unlike Fawkes, was well known to the authorities, and the proclamation against him, a kind of descriptive 'Wanted!' poster, is not so much a mugshot as an intimate portrait. The 'gentleman pensioner' was at this stage the prime lead as Fawkes's pretended master and the man who had rented the vault beneath the Lords' chamber. Though they could deduce some probable plotters from known Catholics suddenly absent from London, the authorities were still relying on the Percy connection to reveal the extent of the plot. It was clear that Percy had regarded his office simply as a vantage point from which to blow the king up. But what of Northumberland, the man who had got him the job? Would he prefer Percy alive or dead?

5 November 1605: Proclamation for the apprehension of Thomas Percy

Whereas one Thomas Percy, a Gentleman Pensioner to his Majesty, is discovered to have been privy to one of the most horrible Treasons that ever was contrived, that is, to have blown up this day, while his Majesty should have been in the upper House of the Parliament, attended with the Queen, the Prince, all his nobility and the Commons, with Gunpowder (for which purpose a great quantity of Powder was conveyed into a vault under the said Chamber, which is this morning there found) the Chamber where they should be assembled, which Percy is sithens fled:

These are to will and command all our Officers and loving Subjects whatsoever, to do that which we doubt not but they will willingly perform according to the former experience we have had of their love and zeal towards us, That is, to make all diligent search for the said Percy, and to apprehend by all possible means, especially to keep him alive, to the end the rest of the Conspirators may be discovered. The said Percy is a tall man, with a great broad beard, a good face, the colour of his beard and head mingled with white hairs, but the head

The final, printed proclamation for the apprehension of Thomas Percy. This equivalent of a 'wanted' poster relied on detailed verbal description to give a clear portrait of the man.

more white than the beard, he stoopeth somewhat in the shoulders, well coloured in the face, long footed, small legged.

Given at our Palace of Westminster, the fifth day of November, in the third year of our reign of Great Britain.

Anno Domini 1605.

Imprinted in London by Robert Barker, Printer to the King's most Excellent Majesty. Anno Domini 1605. (SP 14/73/114–5)

To the government Percy was not just another Catholic malcontent but a betrayer, an insider who had compromised security. Percy's connection with the Earl of Northumberland also made him the government's chief lead in investigating the power behind the plot. The earl, it transpired, had recruited the would-be assassin to guard the king without ensuring he had taken the oath of supremacy obligatory for the job. Not only had Northumberland apparently misjudged Percy's loyalty, but he had also saved him the discomfort of making a statement of it.

Rumours abounded in the first frenetic hours after the discovery of the plot. Percy was reported leaving London in all four compass directions on the same day. However, he was not a lone conspirator fleeing into hiding – a loose end to be tidied up now the immediate danger had passed. On the contrary: the plot had more to it than that. Percy was actually riding as fast as he could to a rendezvous where thousands were expected to join in the next phase. As more information came to light, it began to emerge how Percy had used his official position to ask searching questions about the younger royal children and how they were guarded. Then came reports of horses and arms being stolen close to where the king's elder daughter, the nine-year-old Lady Elizabeth, was staying in Warwickshire. Perhaps the plot had only just begun.

Act II: *Divine Displeasure*

november 1605 to january 1606

CAST LIST

Henry Percy, Earl of Northumberland, captain of the king's bodyguard, 'The Wizard Earl'

Robert Cecil, Earl of Salisbury, Principal Secretary of State, 'The Little Beagle'

William Parker, Lord Monteagle, defender of Catholics in Parliament, recipient of 'The Monteagle Letter'

Anthony Maria Browne, Lord Montagu, nobleman, employer of Guido Fawkes

Sir Everard Digby, gentleman, of Stoke Dry, Rutland and Gayhurst, Buckinghamshire, courtier

Ambrose Rookwood, gentleman, of Coldham Hall, Suffolk, horseman

Francis Tresham, gentleman, of Rushton Hall, Northamptonshire, brother-in-law to Lord Monteagle

Robert Catesby, gentleman, of Ashby St Ledgers, Northamptonshire, and Lapworth, Warwickshire

Robert Wintour, gentleman, of Huddington Court, Worcestershire

Thomas Wintour, gentleman, soldier and scholar, secretary to Lord Monteagle

Thomas Percy, gentleman, member of the king's bodyguard, cousin to the Earl of Northumberland

Stephen Littleton, gentleman, of Holbeach House, Staffordshire

Guido Fawkes, alias Guy Fawkes, alias John Johnson, gentleman, soldier

Henry Garnet, alias Walley, alias Farmer, alias Darcy, Father Superior of the English Jesuit Province

Dudley Carleton, diplomat and social commentator

Francis Bacon, lawyer, philosopher, poet and informer

Ben Jonson, poet, playwright and recusant

Oswald Tesimond, alias Greenway, alias Greenwell, missionary priest, schoolfellow of Guido Fawkes

Edward Oldcorne, alias Hall, missionary priest, schoolfellow of Guido Fawkes

Sheriffs, constables, bailiffs and militiamen

The Hunters and the Hunted

With the first confused reports of a rising in the Midlands, the focus of the plot suddenly widened. The court intrigue of a disillusioned gentleman pensioner abetted by a well-connected gentleman posing as his servant suddenly threatened to become a full-scale Catholic rebellion. Percy was not just a bodyguard turned assassin; he had plotted to kidnap and proclaim a puppet Catholic monarch from among King James's younger children after the explosion. Might part of this plan go ahead though the explosion had been foiled? The authorities were able to draw up an accurate and lengthy list of Catholics suddenly absent from London, compiled by Sir John Popham from his contacts among London's Catholics; all were related and based in the Midlands. The Earl of Salisbury had to rely on reports two or three days old, some accurate, some wild, of what was going on in the Midlands, while the investigations in London brought copious evidence of the plot already foiled but little more on a planned rebellion. The pressure on Fawkes increased, and the authorization to torture him was eagerly taken up by interrogators with an urgent new line of enquiry to pursue. The authorities only got more complete information when the surviving plotters were brought to London on 12 November – whereupon Fawkes's tortured testimony was suddenly overwhelmed by their new evidence. In the week between the discovery of the plot and this date, all was uncertainty, conjecture and confusion. Luckily we can share through the surviving documents not only in the atmosphere of suspicion in London, but also in the rebellion itself.

One of the most memorable scenes in the drama of the Gunpowder Plot must have been the rendezvous on 5 November at Dunchurch in Warwickshire, when Sir Everard Digby's gallant hunting party of Catholic gentlemen was interrupted by the fleeing conspirators from London. They were exhausted and beaten, but Catesby was still proclaiming the king and Salisbury to be dead and a Catholic rising well underway. In a climate where the plotters' only hope of further support lay in maintaining morale, none dared to gainsay him. Digby was taken aside by Catesby and told a series of lies about the success of the venture to keep him on-side. Catesby said 'though he hath been disappointed in his first intention yet was there such a pudder brid [commotion bred] in the state by the death of the King and the earl of Salisbury, as the Catholics would now stir'. Digby might at the time have interpreted this special treatment as a sign of his importance, although gradually his suspicions grew that Catesby was being 'close' and not telling the full truth. Fantasy figures were bandied about, including a force of a thousand supporters expected to converge on Holbeach House in Staffordshire.

Catesby had advised Digby to take a house in Warwickshire or Worcestershire. It was to serve as a base from which to prepare for a hunt on Dunsmore Heath – a front for a raiding party to snatch the Lady Elizabeth, James I's elder daughter, from Coombe Abbey near Coventry. The nine-year-old was to be proclaimed the 'next heir' following the death of her father, brothers Charles Duke of York (the future Charles I) and Prince Henry and assorted Protestant councillors in the explosion in Parliament. Digby duly borrowed Coughton Court from Catesby's cousins, the Throckmortons. He set off for the hunting party, the cover for his mission of abduction, complete with his greyhounds, trunks of money and fine clothes, ready for his role as the reassuring face who would calm the fears of the young princess. Digby was ideally cast as the gallant and handsome knight who would sweep the young girl away from 'captivity', bearing her off on his horse to a new, exciting and romantic life. Controlled by the plotters and their associates, Elizabeth was to become a puppet queen under a Catholic Protector, and in due course a Catholic husband. This pretty illusion overlooked inconvenient realities – not least the fact that the princess was as convinced a Protestant as a girl of her age could be. However, it fuelled Digby's idea of himself as socially indispensable, first to the other conspirators and subsequently, as we shall see, to Salisbury and the wider government.

Digby was a larger than life, heroic character who revelled in his swashbuckling image. John Aubrey (1626–97), author of a brief life of the courtier, called him 'a most gallant gentleman and one of the

PRINCESS ELIZABETH by Robert Peake the Elder, 1603. The plotters' proposed puppet queen, she has a look of resolution and was already a convinced Protestant.

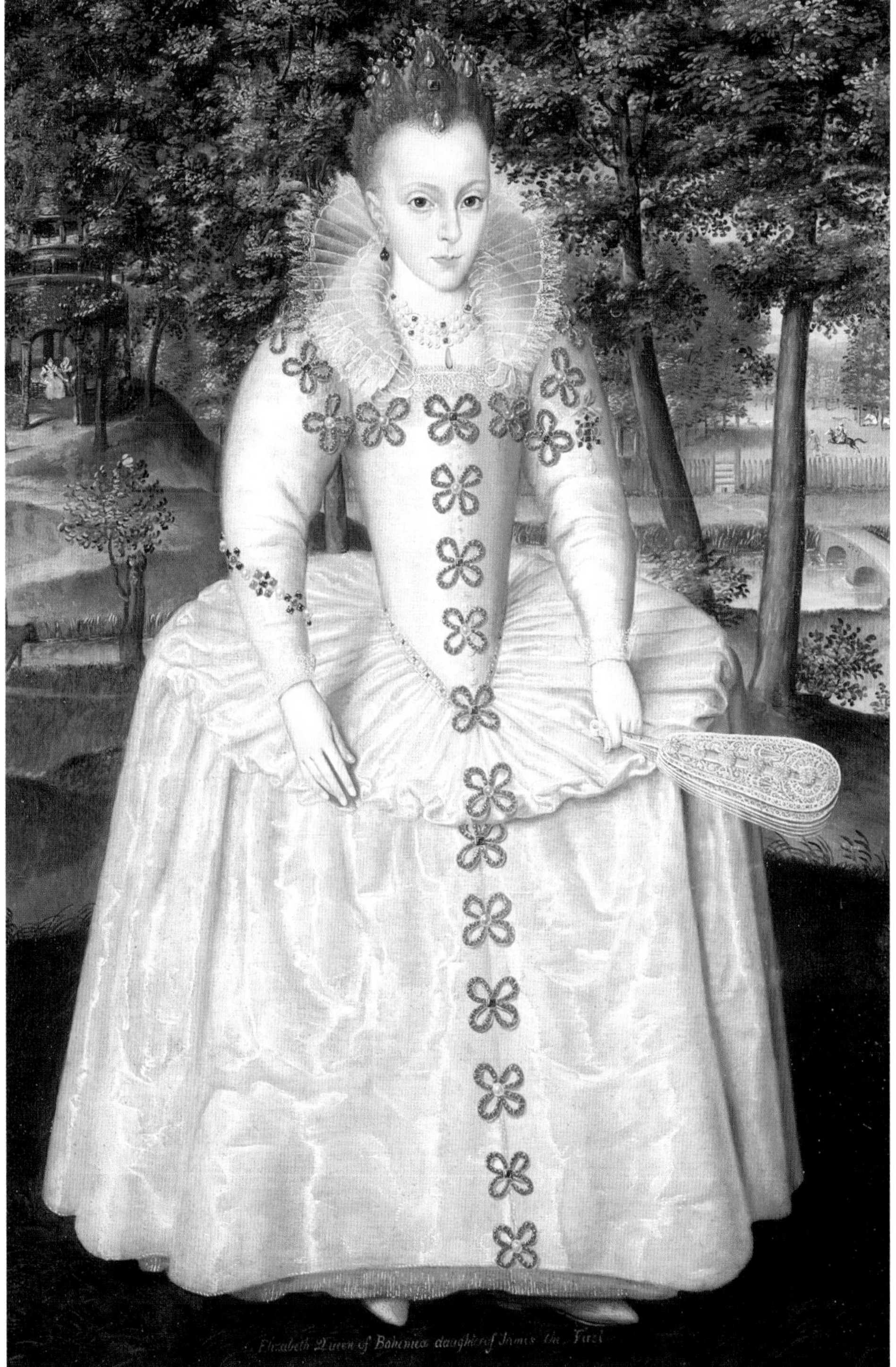
Elizabeth Queen of Bohemia daughter of James the First

handsomest men of his time'. The priest John Gerard, who converted him to Catholicism, also describes him as a handsome man, six feet in height, a complete sportsman, horseman and musician – just the type of man to court the favour and catch the eye of King James. Yet he was manipulated by Catesby into rashness that imperilled his family and was to secure his own destruction.

'This letter only were enough to hang me'

Digby stayed with Catesby, Percy and their associates – some 80 in all. At eleven o'clock on the night of 5 November the rebels raided Warwick Castle, seizing fresh horses from the stables. Such a drastic move was opposed by Thomas Wintour's elder brother, Robert. While his younger brother Tom intrigued with Spain and advertised the plight of English Catholics, Robert Wintour and his wife Gertrude Talbot did their bit for their faith domestically, turning the family home, Huddington in Worcestershire, into a haven for priests. Robert Wintour's letters, written as events unfolded, give us a clear view of a human face among the plotters, from his desperate and unwilling appeal for support to his father-in-law as the Midlands rebellion failed to ignite to revelations of his fearful dreams when a fugitive from justice. He worried about his wife and children, yet was happy to think that they would continue the fight after his death.

With an estate and a family, Robert had more to lose than his brother from a Midlands uprising. His uncharacteristic flirtation with adventure began when he was admitted to the Gunpowder Plot in January 1605 at the Catherine Wheel in Oxford, a haunt of Oxford's Catholic martyrs – at the same time as John Grant and Christopher Wright. The adventure was to cost him his life.

Wintour's connection to the earldom of Shrewsbury through his marriage was a factor in his recruitment, though he himself never seems to have been convinced of the likelihood of any help from his father-in-law. Sir John Talbot of Grafton had had enough trouble with the authorities and was determined to demonstrate his loyalty to King James. Nonetheless, by June 1605 Robert was sending conspiratorial letters to his sister's husband and fellow plotter John Grant in which Talbot's movements were a preoccupation.

After the discovery of the gunpowder end of the operation, Catesby arrived in the Midlands with all his faith pinned on dreams of Talbot's aid. Robert Wintour had stayed in the Midlands and was not among the initial suspects sought by the authorities, but as they trailed from house to house looking in vain for support, he felt the noose begin to tighten around his neck. He spent 6 November very uncomfortably, an unwilling accomplice bound by faith and family to the plotters, but objecting to the 'great uproar in the country' the horse-stealing raid on Warwick Castle would cause, and aware that it would implicate him beyond redemption. Associating with his younger brother, though it would be interpreted as misprision (deliberate concealment) of treason by the authorities, might still be explained away – but the theft of the horses was a deliberate act of rebellion, condemning all that took part.

By the time conspirators arrived at Robert Wintour's house at Huddington, he was its master only in name. Catesby assumed command again and, together with John Wright, pressured his host, who had none of Catesby's illusions about support from Talbot, to write to his father-in-law. As Wintour later protested,

> Mr Catesby and my cousin John Wright took me aside and told me there was no remedy, but I must write to my father [in-law] Talbot to see if I could therewith draw him unto us. I flatly refused it saying, 'My masters, you know not my Father Talbot so well as I. If I should send him such a letter, he would surely stay my man, for I protest I verily think all the world cannot draw him from his allegiance, besides what friends hath my poor wife and children but him, and therefore satisfy yourselves I will not.' 'Well,' (quoth Catesby), 'you shall write to one Mr Smallpeece that serveth your father-in-law.' So to satisfy their importunity I took paper and writ as he willed me word after word, which done, 'Well Sirs,' (quoth I), 'this letter only were enough to hang me and any he that should conceale it.'

The fatal letter that Robert Wintour was forced to write is perhaps a unique survivor from the plot. Neither a strategic plan from before the plot nor evidence generated by the official investigation, it is a hurried note written in desperation and under duress during the rising itself. The possibility that they would all hang preyed on Robert's mind as he wrote, with Catesby dictating and looking critically over his shoulder. Catesby might have reported the incident differently, but the fact remains that Robert Wintour was not prevailed upon to deliver the letter himself; it was found on Thomas Wintour at Holbeach, after he had tried and failed to gain Talbot's support in person. The letter has suffered some damage to the right-hand margin, possibly a result of the injuries sustained by Thomas Wintour at the siege of the house or of events the night before. Though only part of each line survives, the nature and desperation of the plea is very clear.

6 November 1605: A reluctant cry for help – Robert Wintour's letter from Huddington

'A letter found upon [Thomas Wintour] in ye house at Holbeach where he was taken, written to Mr Smallpeece in Mr Talbot of Grafton's house.'
Good cousin I hope it will not seem strange to you that…
a good number of resolved Catholics now perform matters of such…
will set the most straight or hang all those that ever…
use your best endeavour to stir up my father Talbot…
which I should much more honourable than to be hanged after…
cousin pray for me, I pray you and send me all such friends [as thou]
hast, I leave you from Huddington this 6 November' (SP 14/16/19)

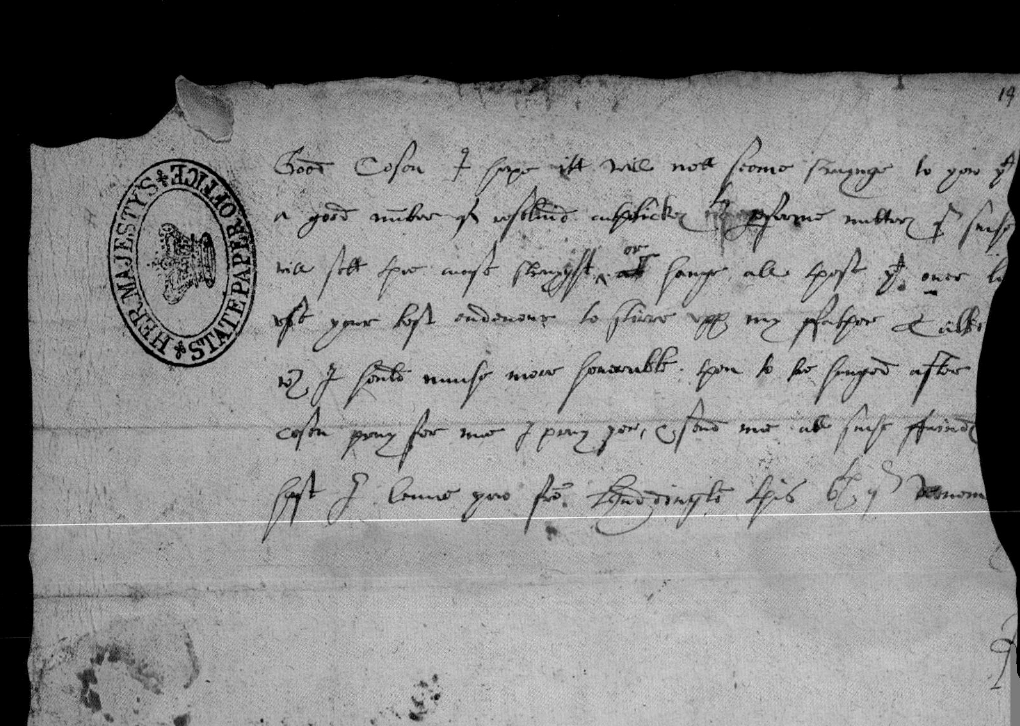

On the same day that Robert Wintour wrote hopelessly to his father-in-law for material aid, Sir Everard Digby wrote to Father Henry Garnet for spiritual support. He was to be equally disappointed. Later, Digby would brag to Salisbury of his influence with Garnet, but when he wrote to the Father Superior on 6 November, asking for pardon and hoping for his support, he received a lecture instead. Garnet wrote back from Coughton saying that he 'marvelled they would enter into so wicked actions, and not be ruled by the advice of friends'. Digby's wife Mary was also at Coughton at the time, and she came upon Garnet and his fellow Jesuit Oswald Tesimond as they discussed her husband's fate with the messenger, Thomas Bate. Garnet recorded that Mary burst into tears when she learned what Digby had done; she knew that he was doomed.

The delivery of the letter, and Garnet's response to it, perfectly sums up his rather ambiguous position. There is no doubt that Garnet was close to and personally sympathetic to the plotters, to the extent that Digby might hope, even if he did not expect, to receive his forgiveness. Yet Garnet did not give it; indeed, his incredulity at their rashness seemed entirely genuine. However, he was staying at Coughton – the house rented by Digby for the meeting at Dunchurch and the Midlands rising – on the day after the king and Parliament were supposed to have been destroyed. The implications were clear, and the priest himself wondered why the authorities were so slow to ask him about this, the strongest piece of circumstantial evidence against him: why, if he were not involved in the plot, did he happen to be there?

Not everyone was engaged in passive wailing and fuelling the sense of doom that fills the examinations taken after the event. There were other fighting spirits as well as the core plotters. Oswald Tesimond, the missionary priest and schoolfriend of Guy Fawkes, had heard of the plot in Catesby's confession in July. On 6 November 1605 he went to the conspirators at Huddington to give the usual consolations of religion. Fellow Jesuit Edward Oldcorne gave

Robert Wintour's incriminating note to Leonard Smallpiece, 6 November 1605. Too much in awe of his father-in-law, Sir John Talbot, to write to him directly, Wintour appealed instead to his steward.

evidence that they had argued when he and Garnet had refused to support the Midlands uprising, and that Tesimond had stormed off, vowing to stir up rebellion in Lancashire. Certainly Tesimond may have been less content with Garnet's caution than Oldcorne was, but it may be that Oldcorne was simply making his own life easier in custody, heaping blame on a man whom he hoped had escaped the authorities.

The Eye of the Storm

As the rebels travelled with varying and lessening degrees of hope from Robert Wintour's house at Huddington to make their final stand at Holbeach, Salisbury was drawing up an account of the plot. This was designed to be read alongside Fawkes's confessions, to inform the Privy Council and then to be published for home and foreign consumption. Piles of documents full of information about the plot, some of it contradictory, much of it useless, poured onto Salisbury's desk in the week between 5 and 12 November. It came from impecunious aristocrats, ambitious lawyers and those bearing local grudges who took the opportunity to establish their own loyalty and sue for reward. However, the still unfolding rebellion meant this account was already well out of date before it emerged.

One of those caught up in the political maelstrom was Dudley Carleton, a rising diplomatic star. After a brief period as secretary to Sir Thomas Parry, ambassador to France, he became controller of the household to Henry Percy, Earl of Northumberland, and through him found a place in the mainstream of court life. At the time Carleton joined Northumberland's household in 1603 the earl, given his role in the succession of James I and restitution by the new king to political significance as a member the Privy Council and a position of trust as captain of the guard, seemed a rising star whose patronage would establish Carleton's own position. By 1605 Carleton was in the Earl of Nottingham's embassy for the ratification of the Anglo-Spanish peace and at the centre of political life. With the Gunpowder Plot and the revelation of the earl's connections with prime conspirator Thomas Percy, all that changed. Worse still, Carleton had been personally involved in obtaining the lease for Thomas Percy of his house next to Parliament and the vault in which the gunpowder was stored.

John Chamberlain, the courtier and 'intelligencer' who wrote news reports in the form of letters, wrote his letter about the plot to Dudley Carleton on the same day that Susan Whynniard, from whom Carleton had helped obtain the lease for Thomas Percy, was examined by the investigating commissioners. He wrote with some sympathetic nervousness about the fate of Carleton's patron, the Earl of Northumberland, but still with a degree of detachment, apparently unaware of how close his friend was to the eye of the storm. Chamberlain's letter was no doubt designed to be comforting to Carleton, but the circumstantial evidence against the earl on the basis of his connection with the prime suspect Thomas Percy sounds damning when spelt out: 'nearness of name, blood, long and inward dependence and familiarity'. However, the mildness of the earl's initial treatment – 'he is rather wished than willed to keep his house' – gave grounds for optimism.

As further news Chamberlain noted 'Sir Edwin Sandys's books burnt. Sir F. Bacon's new work on learning.' The juxtaposition is perhaps significant. Sir Edwin Sandys was in many ways the king's least favourite man, having been prominent among those who opposed the Union of England and Scotland in Parliament and subsequently a major player in the Virginia Company, aiding dissident groups such as the Pilgrim Fathers. It is sometimes said that his book, *A Relation of the State of Religion*, was burnt in the wake of the discovery of the plot because of its tolerant tone towards Catholics, but Chamberlain records that it was burnt in St Paul's churchyard on the Saturday *before* the discovery of the plot.

Francis Bacon was certainly in a more favoured position than Sandys and had spoken in favour of the Union, but he was still outside the charmed circle. Portraits of this complex, highly talented man show a mixture of intellect and slyness; he could seem too good at too many things to be trusted. He might praise James in a poem, but attack royal policy in the House of Commons; or dedicate a great work of philosophy to the king, but undermine his position with legal argument – composed with an artfulness that would escape censure.

By 1605 Bacon had turned to the consolations of philosophy and, having found the usual classical sources unhelpful, written his own. In the long months of the prorogation Parliament, between January and October 1605, while the plotters retired to their houses in the country and waited, Bacon was to write the second book of *The Advancement of Learning*. This book, perhaps the most influential single text in the evolution of scientific method in England, was thought incomprehensible by his hoped-for patron the king; James famously commented that the book was 'like the peace of God which passeth all understanding'. In this experience Bacon the philosopher had something in common with John Donne the satirist, and with many other literary types hoping for advancement at James's court. 'Give me a proper job close to the centre of power,' they seemed to say, 'or I shall write more of this stuff and dedicate it to you.' Bacon had resorted to that most desperate measure, publishing in English, in order to gain an audience. In retrospect he believed that this had been a mistake, and he later published an expanded version in Latin. In the event, any initial impact *The Advancement of Learning* might otherwise have had was thoroughly submerged in the excitement of the discovery of the plot itself.

It was perhaps incumbent on those thought too clever for their own good to make a conspicuous show of loyalty. On the day following Chamberlain's letter, Friday 8 November, Bacon had found another way to put himself forward; he became part of the Earl of Salisbury's network of intelligence. The Inns of Court, where Bacon began and ended his career, were essential breeding grounds for the clever lawyers the government needed to present its version of events and prosecute so many peripheral figures on circumstantial evidence. Yet they were also self-sufficient, independent institutions, said to harbour Catholic priests and sympathizers, and a hotbed of seditious rumours. It was from here, in the frenetic days

A PORTRAIT of Francis Bacon by Paul van Somer. To his celebrated talents as a philosopher, poet, lawyer and statesman, Bacon added the roles of informer and investigator in relation to the plot. His *Essays* are perhaps the finest literary example of how to say two contradictory things at once, a technique common to the plot documents.

The exam of Jo: Drake servant to Th. Reynolls Shoomaker dwelling in Holborn near Grays Inne gate taken the 6 of November 1605

He saith that the morning of this present day he repaired to the lodging of one Mr Boarde in the house of one Gibson in ffetter lane end against the new Church yard, to take measure for new Bootes, and it was in the morning about seven of the clocke and finding him a bedd, mr Boarde asked him what there were stirring and walking abroad, to wch this examinate sayd that the night before there was much stirring and searching for Papists and recusants and namely one Percy.

And this exam sayd further that it was the most heinous Treason that ever was wch was intended to wch the said Boarde sayd He had been brave sport yf it had gone forwards and this speache he spake as muttering to himself, so as the last words were scant heard, and not in any laughing or jesting manner, yet afterwards the said Boarde spake against the fact very much.

The sayd Reynolls being present at this exam saith that he hath served the said Boarde of Bootes these two yeares before and that he used to lodge at Mrs Vaghans house in at the upper end of St Jones Streete who is reported to be a recusant and to bring up recusants children wch are there to learn, but removed to Gibsons house about half a yeare agon.

John Drake

The marke of Th. Reynolls

Exa per Fra: Bacon

after the discovery of the plot, that Bacon got his information and chose to pass it on to Salisbury. He enclosed an explanatory note:

> I send an examination of one [who] was brought to me by the principal ... of Staple Inn today, the words of one Beard, suspected for a papist and practiser, being general words, but bad and I thought not good to neglect any thing at such a time.

Bacon enclosed with this note a witness statement, which conveys something of the atmosphere of celebration and suspicion prevailing two days earlier, the Wednesday morning after the discovery of the plot. The searches among London Catholics, which allowed Sir John Popham to determine the principal conspirators very quickly, created a fearful, dog-eat-dog atmosphere in which a boot-maker could turn on a long-standing customer.

Bacon has signed this witness statement, which was evidently made on the same day as the incident, being 'the examination of John Drake servant to Thomas Reynolds shoemaker dwelling in Holborn near Gray's Inn'. Drake went to Mr Beard's lodging in the house of one Gibson in Fetter Lane to take measure for a new pair of boots. After Beard asked about the 'watching and warding' on the streets and the searches of Catholic houses for plot suspects, Drake heard him mutter under his breath 'it had been brave sport, if it had gone forwards'. Not, as Drake said, 'in any laughing or jesting manner' – so presumably satire on the desirability of blowing up politicians was something he would recognize – but something more sinister. Drake added that Beard afterwards 'spoke against the [plot] very much', implying bluster to cover his indiscretion, perhaps sensing Drake's sense of humour failure. More witnesses were swiftly found to testify that Beard had previously lodged with a known recusant who 'hath bought up recusant children', a still greater offence. No evidence is taken from Beard himself, who no doubt could expect his own visit from the authorities.

Bacon's reward for his loyalty was to be made one of the lesser commissioners who investigated the wives, servants and minor

The witness statement supplied to Salisbury by Francis Bacon on 8 November 1605, providing evidence of careless talk about the plot on the morning after its discovery (SP 14/16/291).

conspirators suspected of involvement in the Gunpowder Plot. Meanwhile the Lords Commissioners, headed by Salisbury himself, dealt with the lords, priests and gentlemen. Once again Bacon had achieved a level of official recognition somewhat below his own estimation of his abilities.

Ben Jonson, a familiar figure beside Francis Bacon in the literary history of the period, appeared alongside Bacon, also providing evidence relating to the plot which was received by the Earl of Salisbury's on the same day. Jonson, too, was giving evidence of a sort about London's Catholics – perhaps the consequence of a deal to obtain his release from prison in the summer of 1605, when he and fellow playwrights were imprisoned following the perfomance of their satiric play *Eastward Ho!* at Blackfriars.

Whether he was continuing to live on the wrong side of the law, or had entered into secret government business as an informer, Jonson found himself in the autumn near the heart of the plot. He attended a supper party on or about 9 October 1605 at William Patrick's house, 'The Irish Boy' in the Strand. Here were found many of the leading conspirators and suspects, who had returned to London in anticipation of the new session of Parliament: Robert Catesby, Francis Tresham, Thomas Wintour, Lord Mordaunt and Sir Jocelyn Percy, brother of the Earl of Northumberland and yet another participant in Essex's revolt of 1601.

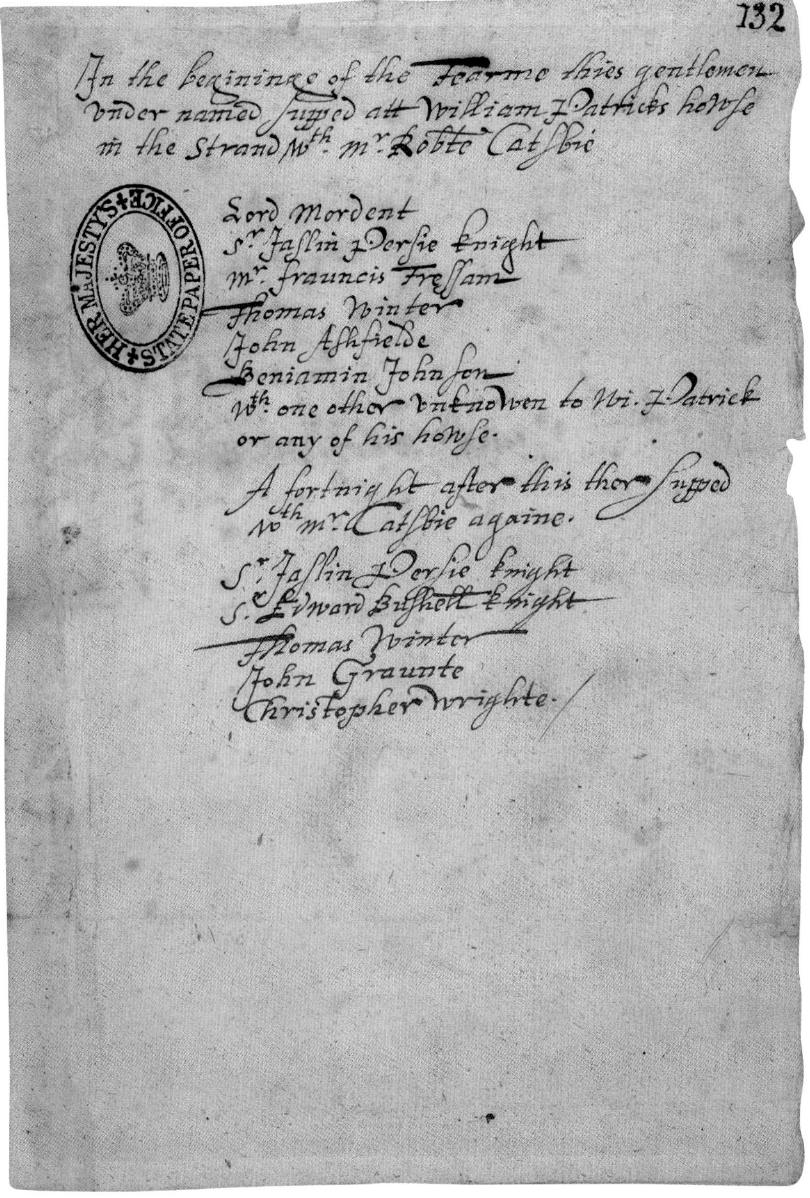
132

In the beginninge of the Tearme thies gentlemen
vnder named supped att William Patricks howse
in the Strand wth mr Robte Catsbie

HER MAJESTY'S STATE PAPER OFFICE

Lord Mordent
Sr Josslin Persie knight
mr ffrauncis Tressam
Thomas Winter
John Ashfielde
Beniamin Johnson
wth one other vnknowen to Wi. Patrick
or any of his howse.

A fortnight after this they supped
wth mr Catsbie againe.

Sr Josslin Persie knight
Sr Edward Bushell knight
Thomas Winter
John Graunte
Christopher wrighte.

A contemporary woodcut (left), showing vintners in a Tudor alehouse. Alehouses were valuable meeting places in an age of little domestic privacy. Informers vied to supply lists of suspects (above). This one includes the key plotters, plus Francis Tresham, Lord Mordaunt and Ben Jonson (SP 14/216/132).

My most honorable Lord.

May it please yor Lo: to vnderstand, there hath bene no want in mee, eyther of labor or sincerity in the discharge of this busines, to the satisfaction of yor Lo: and the State. And whereas, yesterday, vpon the first Mention of it, I tooke the most ready Course (to my present thought) by the Venetian Ambassadors Chaplin, who not only apprehended it well, but was of mind wth mee, that no Man of Conscience, or any indifferent Loue to his Countrey would deny to doe it; and withall engaged himselfe to find out one, absolute in all Numbers, for the purpose; wch he will'd me (before a Gent: of good Credit, who is my Testimony) to signifie to yor Lo: in his Name: It falls out since, that that Party will not be found, (for soe he returnes answere.) Vpon wch I haue made attempt in other Places, but can speake wth no one in Person (all being eyther remoou'd, or so conceal'd, vpon this present Mischeife) but by second Meanes, I haue receaued answere of doubts, and difficulties, that they will make it a Question to the Archpriest, wth other such like suspensions: So that to tell yor Lo: playnly my heart, I thinke they are All so enweau'd in it, as it will make 500 Gent: lesse of the Religion wthin this weeke, if they carry theyr vnderstanding about them. For my selfe, if I had bene a Preist, I would haue put on wings to such an Occasion, and haue thought it no aduenture, where I might haue done (besides his Maiesty, and my Countrey) all Christianity so good seruice. And so much I haue sent to some of them.

If it shall please yor Lordsh: I shall yet make farder triall, and that you cannot in the meane time be prouided: I doe not only wth all readynesse offer my seruice, but will performe it wth as much integrity, as yor particular Fauor, or his Maiesties Right in any Subiect he hath, can exact.

Yo^r Ho: most perfect
seruant and Louer
Ben: Jonson.

This reminder of Jonson's involvement landed on the Earl of Salisbury's crowded desk on 6 November, nearly a month after the event, along with a plethora of half-remembered and possibly invented information from people wishing to ingratiate themselves with the authorities in the wake of the discovery of the plot. On the very next day, Jonson received a warrant from the Privy Council allowing him to escort an unnamed priest to visit the Lords, and give testimony about the conspiracy to members of the council. Jonson proved to be quick but unsuccessful in his work; by Friday 8 November he was reporting his failure to locate this priest – possibly the Jesuit who converted Jonson some years earlier.

8 November 1605: Ben Jonson and the disappearing Catholics – letter to the Earl of Salisbury

May it please your Lordship to understand, there hath been no want in me, either of labour or sincerity in the discharge of this business to the satisfaction of your Lordship or the state. And whereas yesterday upon the first mention of it I took the most ready course (to my present thought) by the Venetian Ambassador's chaplain, who not only apprehended it well, but was of mind with me, that no man of conscience or any indifferent love to his country would deny to do it, and withal engaged himself to find out one, absolute in all Numbers, for the purpose, which he willed me (before a gentleman of good credit who shall be my testimony) to signify to your Lordship in his name. It falls out since that that Party will not be found (for so he returns answer) upon which I have made attempt in other places, but can speak with no one in person (or being either removed or so concealed upon this present mischief) but by second means I have received answer of doubts and difficulties, that they will make it a Question to the Archpriest with such other like suspensions: so that to tell your Lordship plainly my heart; I think they are all so enweaved in it as it will make 500 gentlemen less of the Religion within this week if they carry their understanding about with them. For myself if I had been a priest I would have put on wings to such an Occasion and have thought it no adventure where I might have done (besides his Majesty and my country) all

Jonson's long letter to the Earl of Salisbury, dated 8 November 1605, deploys considerable literary art. His expressions of loyalty produce no evidence and commit him to nothing.

Christianity so good service. And so much have I sent to some of them. If it shall please your Lordship I shall not make further trial and that you cannot in the mean time be provided I do not only with all readiness offer my service, but will perform it with as much integrity as your particular favour, or his Majesty's right in any subject he hath, can exact. Ben Jonson (SP 14/16/30)

It is difficult not to feel that this letter is even more ambiguous and opaque than it need be. In essence, Jonson confesses that he has achieved nothing and will do nothing more unless Salisbury insists, but he takes a very long time, and lot of qualifying remarks in brackets, to say it. In the end, perhaps, it does reveal something about the atmosphere among Catholic priests in London and Jonson's own religious position. Theoretically no Catholic priests were allowed in London, but there were evidently sufficient numbers in the capital to merit a network of spies. Before the plot, Salisbury clearly had a number of contacts among them. The government was prepared to deal with 'loyal' priests in return for information, and the latter, negotiating the shark-infested waters of belief and patriotism, appeared relatively willing to give it. Jonson's line about consulting the Archpriest implies a degree of confusion among London's frightened and fugitive Catholics as to what a good Catholic ought to do following the discovery of the plot. Characteristically, Jonson follows a standard satiric Protestant line about Catholics abandoning their 'politically inconvenient' religion in the wake of the plot (hardly fair, given the actual privations many suffered daily for it) with a thought about how he would behave if he were a priest himself. Evidently this was not so great an imaginative leap.

Jonson's attitude seems even more ambiguous in the light of events that followed. On 10 January 1606, while Sir Edward Coke was preparing the case against Sir Everard Digby and just a few days after the performance at court of one of Jonson's masques – surely a sign of royal favour – Ben and his wife Anne Jonson were presented before the consistory court on charges of recusancy. Jonson

A DETAILED ACCOUNT of the discovery of the plot, with amendments by Salisbury, 7 November 1605. The official 'clarification' of Lord Monteagle's actions and motivations had begun (SP 14/216/129).

Before the Kings Matis comming from Royston, there was a letter delivered to the Lo: Mounteglés footman, as he passed in the streete towards night, directed to his Lord by a party unknowne, written in a hand disguised wthout date, or name, whereof these were the Contents.

My Lord, out of the love I beare to some of yor frends. &c.

As soone as he had read it, and observed the same, he resolved in his Mats absence, to impart it to some of his Mats privy Councell, not so much in respect of any great credit his Lp gave to the letter, as because he tooke himself bound in duty, to make all things any way concerning the Kings person or state, in honor, or safety, knowne to his Maty, either by himself immediately, or by some of those, to whom the consideration thereof did more properly belong: for which purpose he repaired to Whitehall to the Erle of Salisbury his Mats principall Secretary, whom he found in the Company of the Lo: Admirall, the Erle

of

claimed that he had not taken communion because of a religious 'scruple', and so was ordered to discuss his theological difficulties with the Dean of St Paul's and the Archbishop of Canterbury's chaplain. Their arguments cannot have been too persuasive because in May and June of the same year he and Anne were back in the consistory court to answer the same charges.

Jonson prudently directed a congratulatory epigram to Lord Monteagle, whom he praised as the 'saver of my country'. Perhaps a more genuine response emerged in the more ambiguous form of his next play, *Volpone*, written and performed in the early months of 1606. Whether or not he was influenced by his negotiations with the Venetian embassy at the time of the plot, the play is set in Venice. Italian settings, beloved of Shakespeare and Jonson, gave an opportunity for playwrights to show their audiences Catholicism as the accepted religion of the country, or to satirize it. *Volpone* depicts a Venice under the influence of St Mark, the patron saint of goldsmiths, in which the worship of money has long since replaced religion, and his audience might well recognize the governing greed of London underlying this exotic setting. Whatever his religious views, Jonson remained a consistent victim of Stuart patronage. He subsisted on royal pensions rarely paid, alternately rewarded meagrely for his wit and imprisoned for his indiscretions.

This mass of London information was all very well, but the authorities also needed to know urgently about the Midlands rising and plans to kidnap and proclaim 'the next heir'. Their only direct source of information was still Guy Fawkes, who was examined again on Friday 8 November 1605. However, he would – or perhaps could – tell them little more than they already knew:

> as they knew not how to seize Prince Charles, they resolved to surprise the Princess Elizabeth, and make her queen; they prepared, in her name, a proclamation against the Union of the Kingdoms, and in justification of their act, but without any declaration as to religion; they would have taken the [English-born] Princess Mary, but knew not how.

They also tried to establish the nature of the rebels' plans by examining royal servants who had seen Thomas Percy acting suspiciously and asking questions about the royal children in the days before the discovery of the plot. On the same day Fawkes was examined, one Agnes Fortun was able to shed more light on their inability to 'seize Prince Charles' (later Charles I). Entitled 'A report of a Scottish woman concerning Percy', it sounds unpromising, as if it had been hastily labelled 'more gossip' by a weary official. However, this does in fact provide telling and dramatic evidence of Thomas Percy's role in the plot.

Fortun was a servant to Charles and recalled a conversation in which Percy had been keen to know the prince's routine and how he was guarded. The testimony of Fawkes, and other evidence relating to the 'hunt' at Dunchurch, suggests they had settled on 'the Lady Elizabeth' as their puppet monarch, having now abandoned the possibility of taking Prince Charles. Perhaps Percy's interview with Agnes Fortun was the final nail in the coffin of the former plan, which was then abandoned. Not only was the prince well protected at all times, but the staircase by which Percy had hoped to surprise him had recently been blocked to 'make his chamber more private'. Fortun had offered Percy the chance to stay and see both Charles and the man charged with protecting him – 'if he would stay a bonny while he might see the Duke [of York] and Sir Robert Carey both' – but Percy declined this offer and left, still looking hard at the blocked staircase and contemplating a change of plan.

The other tactic of the authorities on 8 November was to set rebel against rebel by singling out Percy and offering a reward for his apprehension. Once again, however, events in the Midlands were to overtake them.

'Hoist with their own petard'

After a dispiriting trudge in cold drizzle, which had failed to raise a single supporter but allowed many of those who had rallied at Dunchurch to make their escape, the 14 remaining rebels arrived at Holbeach House, Staffordshire, on the evening of 7 November. They decided to dry their damp – currently useless – gunpowder before the open fire, only for the large stocks (designed to equip an army which never materialized) to explode. In the aftermath of the disaster, Catesby and Rookwood emerged badly burned and John Grant almost blinded. The others were badly shaken, and any remaining confidence was swiftly eroded. This horrific explosion, rich in dramatic irony, finally roused fear in the conspirators' minds that God did not, after all, support their scheme. John Wright suggested to Catesby they might take this signal of divine displeasure as a cue to end their hopeless situation by blowing themselves up completely with the remaining gunpowder – an intriguing deviation from strict Catholic theology. The suggestion was not followed, but unsurprisingly there were further desertions.

One of the most significant departures was that of Sir Everard Digby. He rode off with two servants early the following morning, 'deserting' Holbeach before the inevitable siege – a desperate action perhaps prompted by the need to escape Catesby's web of words and find out what was actually going on. Digby's instinct was to try to find someone of sufficient rank to surrender to, but he found no one. He tried to hide in a wood, but was tracked by his horse's hoof marks to a dry ditch. The pursuing sheriff's men crowed at their discovery, crying 'Here he is, here he is', but Digby, too proud and too confident to stay in hiding, rode out with a challenge: 'Here he is indeed, what then?' At first he hoped to break through his pursuers, but, recognizing at last the overwhelming odds, he surrendered.

Digby was taken to London and lodged with the other superior prisoners in the Tower. Initially, he denied all knowledge of the plot before his conversation with Catesby on 5 November, but, confronted with the evidence of Guy Fawkes and Thomas Wintour, he eventually admitted his deeper involvement.

Wintour's own story is vividly recaptured in documents of the time, and through his evidence the final, fatal twists of the plot fall into place. On the morning of 8 November, carrying his brother Robert's unwilling plea for support, he had ridden to Pepper Hill and called on Sir John Talbot in a vain attempt to recruit assistance. Returning from the fruitless mission, Wintour was advised by Stephen Littleton (one of the plotters and the owner of Holbeach House) while still some distance from Holbeach to make good his

SPECIAL DEPOSITIONS taken by Commission at Worcester and Stafford describe Thomas Wintour's capture at Holbeach. Local forces besieging the plotters disputed among themselves who had taken Wintour prisoner (see transcription p.93).

Depositions of Witnesses taken before Sr Ric Lewson knight James Sutton esquier and Nicholas Bowyer gent in Hartlebury in the County of Worcester the xviijth day of June Anno Regni Jacobi et Anglie Francie et Hibernie tertio et Scotie xxxixno by vertue of a Comission forth of his Maties Court of Exchequer to them and others directed

Gilbert Wheeler of Droytwich in the County of Worcester gent of the age of xxxij yeares or thereabouts sworne and examined on the pte behalfe saith and deposeth as followeth

To the first inter he saith that he hath knowne the plt for some yeare and a quarter, And the deft but sithens Fryday last to his remembrance.

To the second he saith that the Compt was ensigne bearer unto Sr Fraunces Wallshe, at the tyme of the service in the inter mentioned

To the third this dept saith that beinge then in the saide service at Holbeach he did see the Compt first of any man to his knowledge leape on the wall of the Court of Holbeach And presently after did see the Compte shoote Thomas Wynter by one arme with two naked swords in the other of his hands One of which the Compt afterwards sayed was Thomas Wynters swords And in his conscience he is verely pswaded that he the Compt did as good service as any one man in the Companye did that daye, both in the apprehension and savinge of the life of the said Thomas Wynter.

To the vith inter this dept saith that upon the vith day of November Thomas Wynter amongst other the Traytors was brought to the towne hall of Worc and at that tyme havinge a paire of guilt boote spurres on his heeles, the officers of the towne intendinge to have pulled of his bootes, would have taken away his spurres, as due unto them, but the Compt William beinge their present made open challenge of the said spurres as he sayed due to him, by the lawe of Armes for that he first apprehended him the said Wynter and tooke him prisoner which words were spoken in the hearinge and view of the said Wynter, Whereupon the said spurres were yeilded to the said Compt accordingly

Robert Barret of Droytwich in the County of Worc gent of the age of xlij yeares or thereabouts sworne and examined saith and deposeth as followeth

To the first inter he saith that he hath knowen the plt aboute a yeare and a quarter last past, and the deft not above three dayes last past.

To the third vi and last inter he saith that he sawe Thomas Wynter the Compt leape on the wall of the Court of Holbeach And this dept is verylie pswaded in his conscience the Compt was the first man that first entred the said Court he this dept standinge in a place where he might well observe the same

Ja: Sutton

N Bowyer

escape. Wintour later recorded his soldierly response. 'I told him I would first see the body of my friend and bury him, whatsoever befell me.' In his own account, Wintour asked Catesby, Percy, the Wrights, Rookwood and Grant what they meant to do. 'They answered, we mean here to die. I said again I would take such part as they did.' When the house was besieged by the local militia on the Friday morning, Thomas Wintour, Robert Catesby and Thomas Percy – the bachelor, the widower and the bigamist – fought back to back in a last desperate struggle. Only Wintour survived long enough to report their last stand:

> Then said Mr Catesby to me standing before the door they were to enter, 'Stand by me, Tom, and we will die together.' 'Sir,' quoth I, 'I have lost the use of my right arm and I fear that will cause me to be taken.' So as we stood close together Mr Catesby, Mr Percy and my self they two were shot (as far as I could guess) with one bullet, and then the company entered upon me, hurt me in [the] belly with a pick and gave me other wounds until one came behind and caught hold of both mine arms.

Documents also survive which give us an account of the siege from the point of view of the besieging forces. They provide intriguing insight into the nature of local law enforcement. Those who joined specially raised forces might do so with their own loyalties and motivations. Among those who joined the force of Charles Blount, Earl of Devonshire, charged with putting down the rebellion, was Francis Tresham, characteristically seeking his own credit. Such local forces were also prone to disputes among the sheriffs of the individual counties when the action took place, as at Holbeach, on the border of three counties.

Our most dramatic first-hand account of the capture of Thomas Wintour comes from evidence taken from a dispute among local militias. Men under the command of Sir Francis Kettleby and Sir Richard Walsh haggled about who was responsible for taking Thomas Wintour prisoner. One (Thomas Williams) had sought to preserve his life, and the other (Thomas Bannister) would have killed him; both claimed him as their prisoner. The document preserves a version of the dialogue of the fight and reveals the deference and social sensitivity of the militia in the presence of gentlemen, albeit treacherous ones, which reads strangely to modern ears.

8 November 1605: Account of Thomas Wintour's capture at Holbeach

Interrogatories administered on behalf on the complainant [Williams] to the defendant [Bannister] 'Did you not see the complainant Williams leap down into the court of Holbeach first and before any man and did you hear the complainant say to Wintour 'Gentleman, yield' and did not Wintour say 'Kill me and I will kill thee if I can' and did you not thrust at Wintour with your bill and did not the complainant Williams break your thrust with his calliber and say 'Oh hurt him not!' and did not you say to some of your friends and acquaintance, that on your conscience you had killed the said Wintour if the complainant Williams had not been there. (E 134/4JAS I/TRIN 6)

Williams, it seems, took Wintour's 'damask sword' and handed it to Bannister to free his hands while he secured the prisoner. Bannister later used the sword as evidence that he had taken Wintour prisoner. In an interesting postscript, the same document includes the evidence of Gilbert Wheeler of Droitwich, who describes how when Thomas Wintour was taken as a prisoner to Worcester a dispute arose over his spurs:

… a pair of gilt copper spurs on his heels the offices of the town intending to have pulled off his boots would have taken away his spurs as due unto them, but the complainant Williams being there present made open challenge of the said spurs being due to him as he said by law of arms. (E 134/4JAS I/TRIN 6)

The argument was apparently heard in Wintour's presence, and Williams' prior claim upheld. It offers further minor evidence of the cost and style of the plotters' clothing and arms. At the same time the investigator Sir William Waad was preoccupied with significantly embroidered scarves made for the conspirators, and there were also examinations of a cutler who had made them swords engraved with Christ's passion. These might simply be for their protection, but they also suggest a group dressed for martyrdom.

Confessions and Conspiracies

While the rebellion was petering out a hundred miles away, Guy Fawkes in the Tower was coming under increasing pressure from the authorities to tell all he knew. He was no longer a source of information merely about a plot whose danger had passed, but about what appeared to be a present and uncertain danger. In such a climate England's Grand Inquisitor, Sir William Waad, wrote to his master the Earl of Salisbury with clear indications that at the very least some of 'the gentler tortures' specified in the king's letter of 6 November were being threatened. The severity of this treatment reflected the scale of the government's anxiety. Wild rumours were still being received about the extent of the Midlands rebellion, suggesting a growing popular uprising that might threaten the government afresh.

9 November 1605: Waad reports that Fawkes is ready to divulge 'the secrets of his heart'

I have prevailed so much at the length with my prisoner, by plying him with the best persuasions I could use as he hath faithfully promised me by narration to discover to your lordship only all the secrets of his heart, but not to be set down in writing. Your lordship will not mislike the exception, for when he hath confessed himself to your lordship, by degrees I will undertake he shall acknowledge it before such as you shall call, and then he will not make dainty to set his hand with it. Therefore it may please your good lordship, if any of the Lords do come with you, that first your lordship will deal with him alone. He will conceal no name nor matter from your lordship to whose ears he will unfold his bosom. And I know your lordship will think it the best journey you ever made upon so evil occasion. Thus in haste, I thank God my poor labour hath advanced a service of this importance. From the Tower of London, the 9th of November, 1605.

At the commandment of your Lordship W.G. Waad (SP 14/216/53)

When Fawkes did set his hand to the declaration which followed, he could barely write. The infamous declaration with its failing signature in fact gave the authorities little additional information. Fawkes told less under torture than had already been provided by Thomas Wintour, now held in government hands at Worcester;

William waad's report to Salisbury, 9 November 1605. Fawkes seems to have resisted making a written confession; when he finally 'acknowledged' a written version of his verbal confession, he could barely write.

My honorable good L. I haue preuayled so much at the lenthe wth my prisoner by plying him wth the best perswations I could vse, as he hathe faythfully promised me by narration to discouer to yr L. only all the secrets of his hart, but not to be set down in writing, yr L. will not mislyke the exception, for when he hathe confessed him self to yr L. by degrees I will undertake he shall acknowledge it before such as you shall Call, and then he will not make dainty to set his hand vnto it. Therfore it may please yr L. if any of the LLs do come wth you shall first yr L. will deal wth him alone, he will conceale no name nor matter from yr L. whose eares he will vnfold his Bosome, And I know yr L. will thinke it the best Jorney you euer made vpon so small occasion. Thus at last I thanke God my poor labor hath aduanced a seruice of this Importance. From the Tower of London the 9th of 9ber 1605.

At the Commandement of yr
ho. L.

W. Waad.

54

The Declaration of Guy Fawkes taken the 9 of 9ber and subscribed by him the 10th day acknowledged before the lords commissioners

A Thomas Winter came over into the Lowe countries unto this Examinate about Easter was twelve monthe, Expresly to break wth him about some Course to be taken for the advauncemt of the Catholike Religion, wch they did communicate to Owen at the campe before and three weeks after this Examinate Came into England in Company of the said Wright, by whose meanes he was made acquainted wth Thomas Percy, Robert Catisby and John wright,

B They five did meete at a Howse in the fields beyond St Clements Inn; where they did Conferr, and Agree, upon the Plott they ment to undertake and put in Execucon; and there they tooke a solemne Oath and vowe by all their force and Power to Execute the same, and of secrecy not to Reveale anie of their fellowes, but to such as should be thought fitt persons to enter into that Accon, And in the same Howse they did receave the Sacrament of Gerrard the Jesuite to performe their vowe, and of secrecy as is aforesaid. But he saith that Gerrard was not acquainted wth their purpose.

C The Plott was to blowe up the Kinge wth all the Nobility about him in Parlament, as heretofore he hathe declared to wch end, they proceeded as is set downe in the Examinacon taken before the LL of the Counsell, Comissioners yesterday the viijte of November; while they followed their [illegible] purpose, there were taken into this Society and Confidence theis persons Vizt. Everet Digby, Robt Keys, Christofer Wright, Thomas Graunt, Francis Tresham Robert Winter, brother to Thomas winter and Ambrose Rookewood

D He further saith that Thomas Percy came to the Towne Expresly to see the Accon put in Execucon, on the saturday at night before the begining of the Parliament, and went out of the Towne information wrested at such human cost from the prisoner was superseded within days by Wintour's arrival in the capital. The rebellion for which Fawkes had suffered was over before he struggled to write his name.

9 NOVEMBER 1605: TOWER DECLARATION OF GUY FAWKES

'The Plot was to blow up the King with all the nobility about him in Parliament … he confesseth also that there was speech amongst them to draw Sir Walter Raleigh to take part with them, being one that might stand them in good stead as others in like sort were named.' [*and signature*] (SP 14/216/54)

THE DECLARATION of Guy Fawkes (left), 9 November 1605. Fawkes's evidence under torture clearly reflected the nature of the questions asked rather than any deeper truth about the plot. Evidence of Fawkes's physical deterioration (below) comes from his very faint signature on the right.

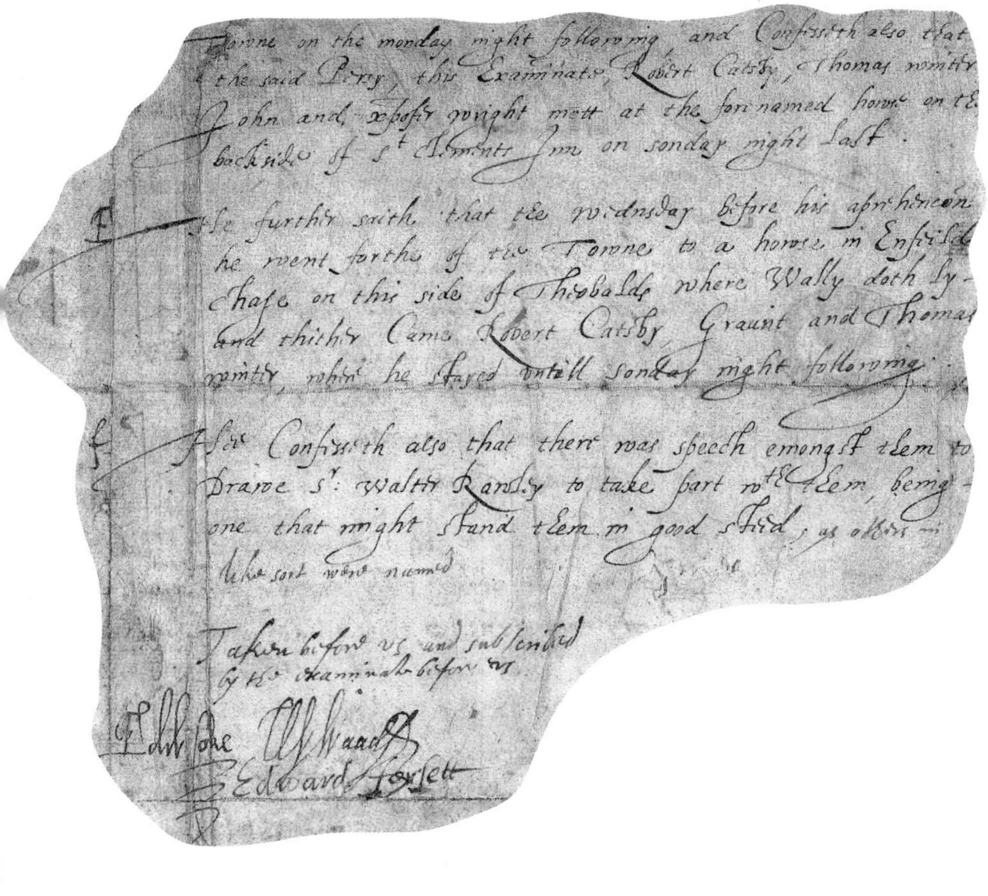
Towne on the monday night following, and Confesseth also that the said Percy, this Examinate, Robert Catsby, Thomas Wintor, John and Christofer Wright mett at the fore named house on the backside of St Clements Inn on sonday night last.

He further saith that the wednesday before his apprehension he went forth of the Towne to a house in Enfield Chase on this side of Thebalds where Wally doth ly, and thither Came Robert Catsby, Graunt and Thomas Wintor, where he stayed untill sonday night following.

He Confesseth also that there was speech emongst them to drawe Sr Walter Rawley to take part with them, being one that might stand them in good stead, as others in like sort were named.

Taken before us and subscribed by the examinate before us

Edw Coke W Waad
Edward Forsett

Fawkes helpfully locates White Webbs, the house rented in Essex by Anne Vaux as a haven for priests where the conspirators often met, in relation to Salisbury's estate, Theobalds. This is not only a declaration made to Salisbury, but to some extent made by him and Coke to reflect their preoccupations – perhaps a sign that evidence under torture was more likely to affirm the questions put than to reveal anything new. On the day before Fawkes's confession, Sir William Waad had identified Francis Tresham, despite his service in the militia, as a 'Spanish pensioner' worth keeping an eye on. Only with Fawkes's confession, however, did Tresham become formally implicated in the plot, albeit as an unwilling figure 'exceeding earnest' to warn Lord Monteagle not to attend Parliament.

Rumours that Thomas Percy had been taken prisoner at Holbeach reached London far enough in advance of the news of his death that Salisbury had the time to report him 'sore hurt and taken' in a letter to Sir Thomas Edmondes in Brussels. The Earl of Northumberland wasted no time in writing a note to the Council dated 'Sunday afternoon' (10 November) that Thomas Percy should be saved if possible from his injuries. Only Percy, if he could be believed, could give the vital evidence that would clear the earl of any complicity. Percy was already dead as he wrote, his injuries sustained on 8 November, exacerbated by ill treatment from 'the baser sort' among the besieging forces, killing him the following day. It is even possible that by Sunday afternoon Northumberland knew this, taking the opportunity to stress his belief in his own innocence in the certain belief that Percy could do nothing to contradict him.

10 November 1605: Saving Thomas Percy's life

I hear Mr Percy is taken, if that I hear be true, but withal shot through the shoulder with a musket; our surgeons in this country are not over excellent for a shot, if heat take it, the patient with a fever will soon make an end; none but he can show me clear as the day, or dark as the night, therefore I hope it shall not offend you if I require haste, for now will he tell only if ever, being ready to make his account to God always. (SP 14/216/225)

Northumberland's letter to the Privy Council, 10 November 1605. Brief and urgent, the earl's note about Percy's health is still full of ambiguity, and his motivations in writing it remain unclear.

May it pleas your Lord: that I haue to say at this tyme is littel, and few words will expresse my desier: not that I am to direct your Lord: wills, but only to lay downe myne owen entreaty if yow like it, and that is this: I heare Mr Percy is taken, if that I here be true, but withall shott throughe the shoulder with a muskett; our surgeans in theas cuntryes are not ouer excelent for a shott, if heat take it, the patient with a febuer will soune make an ende; noen but he can shew me clere as the day, or darke as the night, therefore I hope it shall not offend yow if I requier hast, for now will he tell truely if euer, being ready to make his account to God almighty. Thus with my humble well wishes to your Lord: I rest

to doe your Lord: seruis

Sunday this present afternoone.

As always, Northumberland's note is ambiguous. Perhaps there is an echo, too, in 'clear as the day or dark as the night' of the 'owl-light'/daylight note about Percy in November 1603. Is Percy presented as sincere and religious or insincere and superstitious? The line about Percy's readiness to make confession appears to be a standard Protestant joke at the expense of Catholics obsessed with their own religious practices. In the context of the note, however, it is clear that Northumberland himself believed Percy, despite his treachery, would tell the truth in a deathbed confession. For all his capital temporal offences, Percy would not risk his soul at the last. Such conviction sounds more like a ringing endorsement of Catholic religious practice, a dangerous position for a man trying to prove he was not the hidden power behind Percy's rebellion.

The Earl of Salisbury's agents were soon set to uncover evidence of Jesuit involvement in the plot, in an attempt to show that a supposed Jesuit teaching, which justified the deposition of heretic kings, had influenced the plotters. The confessions of the plotters themselves seemed to suggest that the desire to 'do somewhat in England' came from a simple desire to improve the lot of English Catholics without complex theological justification. Nevertheless, it was politic for the government to suggest that only poisonous indoctrination stopped all Catholics from being loyal 'Church Papists', such as the Earl of Northampton. Accordingly, on 11 November Salisbury received from Thomas Wilson further reports of White Webbs, described as the 'house on Enfield Chase on this side of Theobald's' in Fawkes's declaration. It was still being used as a safe house for priests including Henry Garnet, Superior of the Jesuit Mission in England, not only 'this side of' but also uncomfortably close to Salisbury's estate.

Guy Fawkes might be losing importance to the better informed Thomas Wintour, newly returned to London, but he could still cause trouble through his fashionable connections. One such, Anthony Maria Browne, Viscount Montagu, was a popular Catholic nobleman and a friend of Robert Catesby, portrayed with his brothers by the painter Isaac Oliver as the embodiment of fashionable, self-confident nobility. Montagu's imprisonment for his speeches against anti-Catholic legislation became a focus for Catholic discontent in and outside Parliament. When it emerged that he had employed Guy Fawkes, the circumstantial evidence against him seemed as strong as that against some of the other suspected lords, but Montagu was sufficiently well connected to escape lightly. In cleverly written letters to his father-in-law the Lord Treasurer, Thomas Sackville, Earl of Dorset, Montagu put pressure on him to buy him out of trouble. He skilfully recalled conversations with Catesby in such a way as to involve his powerful relative in his fate.

Dorset asked Montagu to review and clarify his connection with 'the horrible intended treason'. Montagu responded with hints of complicity, as if to say 'I hoped to secure my absence from Parliament through you, so don't forget me,' and rubbed it in by artfully reconstructing Catesby's veiled warning not to attend Parliament in a way that potentially ensnared his father-in-law.

> 'The Parliament I think bringeth up your Lordship now.'
>
> 'No surely but it will upon Monday next, unless my Lord Treasurer do obtain me his majesty's licence to be absent, which I am in some hopes of.'
>
> 'I think your lordship takes no great pleasure there.' Whereunto I assented.

Montagu also expressed a desire to 'speak confidently' (in confidence) to the earl, implying they both had something to hide. The revelation of Fawkes's involvement prompted another letter from Montagu to Dorset in which he put the date of his conversation with Catesby back a week, making it seem less urgent, pressing and conspiratorial, adding

> ... the miserable fellow that should have been the bloody executioner of that woeful tragedy was called Guy Faux. If so were his name he should seem to have been my servant once (though I am sorry to think it) for such a one I had even for some few months, but was dismissed from me by my Lord upon some mislike he had of him.

Days later, Montagu was sent to the Tower. Catesby, it seemed, did have the bravado to play a trick on a few favoured lords who he believed were bright enough to take a hint and wedded enough to him not to betray him. Unlike so many of his fellow prisoners, however, Montagu could be confident of powerful forces working to secure his release.

The Browne Brothers by Isaac Oliver, 1598. Anthony Maria Browne, Lord Montagu (centre), had suffered for his religion, but was also in a position to buy a degree of religious freedom. Debate has raged about the extent of his knowledge of the plot.

The Tentacles of Treason

When the survivors of the siege of Holbeach reached London on 12 November, Salisbury could stop reacting to events and begin investigations in directions of his choosing. The picture was still chaotic, however, and his satisfaction at the success of the government's countermeasures was tinged with unease. The Earl of Northumberland was amicably imprisoned by his fellow Privy Councillor the Archbishop of Canterbury, but was he the real power behind the plot or one of its intended victims, or, as he insisted himself, a man of private life who liked gardening and arcane scientific experiments, with no interest in power? Surely the fact that he had dined with Thomas Percy at Syon House on 4 November was strong circumstantial evidence of his involvement? Reports began to arrive that law enforcement against the rebels had been reluctant in parts of Warwickshire where the Jesuit missionaries had been most successful, that one of those arrested was Sir Everard Digby, a court favourite, that Lord Monteagle was heavily implicated in the plot he had exposed, and that the official version of the plot was being greeted with scepticism abroad.

In some circles, its very existence was doubted. On 13 November Dudley Carleton himself reported from the safety of his diplomatic posting in Paris that the plot was considered a fable in France; he was still commentating with detachment on the plot, apparently unconcerned about his own connection.

> The fire which was said to have burnt our K[ing] and counsel and hath been hot for these two days past in every man's mouth, proves but ignis fatuus or a flash of some foolish fellow's brain, so abuse the world, for it is now confidently reported there was no such matter, nor anything near it more than a barrel of gunpowder found near the court.

Northumberland continued to argue in notes to the Privy Council that he was in no position to play a part in the plotters' plans. The man who little more than two years earlier had been an obvious choice as potential lord protector argued that he was unambitious and given to private pleasures and, crucially, that he had a scanty supply of arms, horses and servants. James and his Council struggled to identify a nobleman sufficiently eminent to serve as protector of the realm had the plot succeeded. The surviving plotters claimed that any decision on the protectorate had been deferred until after the explosion, but again their assurances failed to convince.

At this stage the Earl of Northumberland's detention was still described as a temporary precaution. But suspicion against him grew: no one could quite credit that Percy would have let him die in the Lords. Northumberland was examined by Sir Edward Coke on his role in the plot, again reflecting Coke's twin obsessions: the earl's connections with his friend Sir Walter Raleigh; and treasonable astrology and prophecy in casting of the king's nativity in which Dudley Carleton, then serving in the earl's household, was again implicated. After a lengthy examination on 23 November, Northumberland was dispatched to the Tower four days later.

While Coke the Attorney General followed his own particular lines of enquiry, details from local law officers continued to arrive. An Inquisition into Robert Catesby's lands produced evidence of the hunt for the conspirators on the day before Catesby and Percy made their last stand at Holbeach.

23 November 1605: Searching Moorcrofts

This examinate sayeth that he being the Bailey of the hundred of Elthorne having received one of His Majesty's proclamations for the apprehending of Thomas Percy he forthwith sent to Mr Hawtrey esquire being the next Justice of the Peace for the said county informing him of Catesby's house that it was

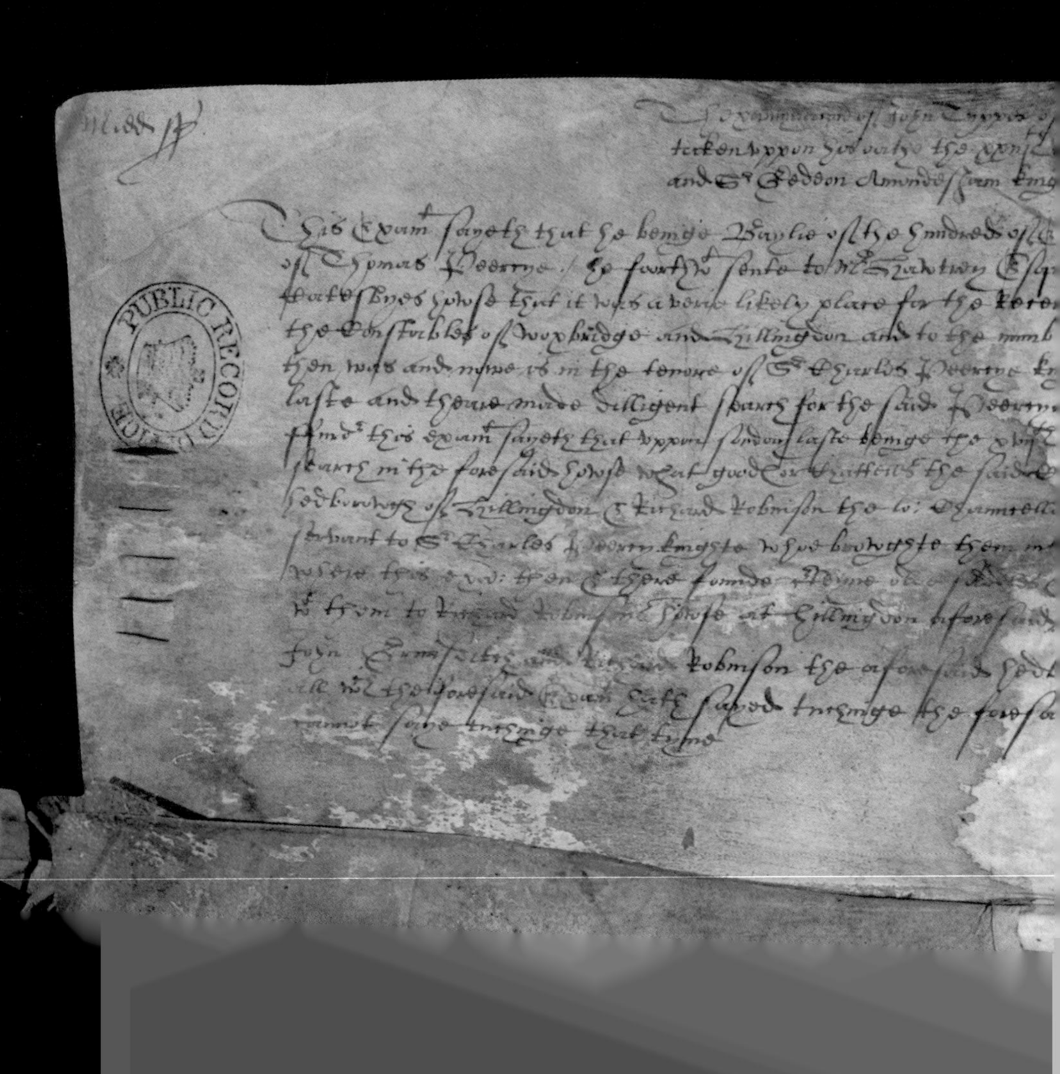

a very likely place for the receipt and harbouring of such persons, who immediately came, [and] with whom this examinate together with the Constables of Weybridge and Hillingdon and to the number of forty persons now went and beset the said Catesby's house called Moorcrofts which then was and now is in the tenure of Sir Charles Percy knight, whereunto the said Justice and Constables entered being the seventh day of November and there made diligent search for the said Percy but could not find him. (E178/4162)

The middlesex county inquisition as to the goods of Robert Catesby, 23 November 1605. Local officers moved quickly on good intelligence to search for Percy at Catesby's house in Hillingdon – as the men faced death in Staffordshire.

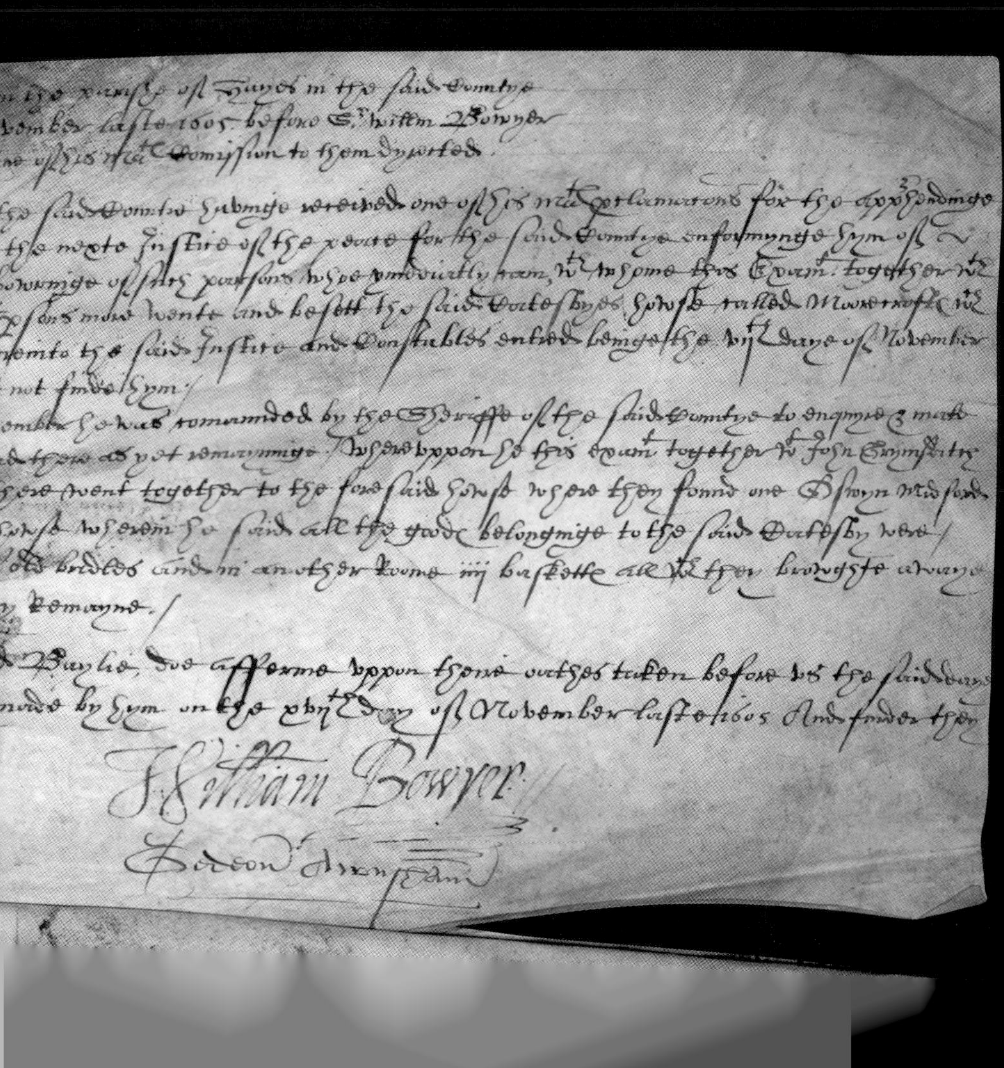

During the day on 7 November, Catesby's house, Moorcrofts at Hillingdon in Middlesex, had been searched by a group of about 40 men, including the local constables, looking for Thomas Percy. Local intelligence about Catesby's house and his likely visitors was very good, although as always this did not always permeate through to the investigation's heart. John Tupper, a local bailiff, receiving the proclamation against Thomas Percy of 5 November, went to the local justice of the peace to say that they were very likely to find Percy at Catesby's house where he had undoubtedly been many times. They had no means of knowing that Percy and Catesby were within hours of dying together a hundred miles away, or even, it seems, that Catesby himself was involved.

On 18 November the search was renewed and Catesby's goods at Moorcrofts confiscated. There they found Owen Midford, servant to Northumberland's brother Sir Charles Percy, who had lived at Moorcrofts rent-free for several months before taking a lease of the place in 1605.

Catesby's servant Yeomans came to Richard Robinson, another local officer, on Tuesday 19 November. He claimed that he had hidden £54 in money in a cloak bag in one of the outbuildings at Moorcrofts where the saddles and bridles were, to avoid the search; when he came back, he found the bag but the money was gone. Yeomans added, with the suspicious air of a man making an insurance claim, that £34 of this money was his own, and only the residue belonged to Catesby! The cook of the house was suspected of the theft, having been suddenly 'very desirous to go to London', and was in due course tracked down there by Robinson and Yeomans – very efficient but slapstick at the same time. Out of this document too emerged evidence that Catesby had used the house as a base from which to travel to Royston where the king had been hunting in the weeks before the discovery of the plot.

In many ways, Catesby's particular personality – charismatic but desperate – shaped the plot and made it difficult for the investigating authorities to understand. All their instincts and every precedent told the investigators that it was highly unlikely that the plotters would act without popular support, the patronage of an aristocrat or foreign aid. In fact, such a lone attempt was very characteristic of

Catesby, his ability to persuade and motivate balanced by impatience with those he could not control. What evidence would he have given his interrogators had he not been killed in the siege at Holbeach? No doubt he would have treated the assembled councillors as if they were his captive audience, rather than the other way around. Would he have regaled them with grand plans and links to 'great men' and foreign powers, which he had kept 'close', even from the other conspirators? So many of the leads followed by the investigators seemed to be based on hints from evidence about Catesby. Would he have substantiated these, or simply convinced the authorities that the plotters had indeed acted alone and a wider rebellion was simply the product of Catesby's fevered imagination?

In the Shadow of the Plot

Perhaps fortunately, the authorities now had in their hands a historian of the plot less wild, boastful and vain than Catesby or Percy, a man who had reported his role in the bloody conflict in the Low Countries with an ironic detachment which he now brought to his role in the plot: Thomas Wintour. On 23 November Sir William Waad wrote to Salisbury of the financial concerns of his prisoners in the Tower: well-connected Rookwood deserted by his rich friends and Digby with trunks of money in London, complaining that the sheriff of Warwickshire had taken £100 from him. He also reported

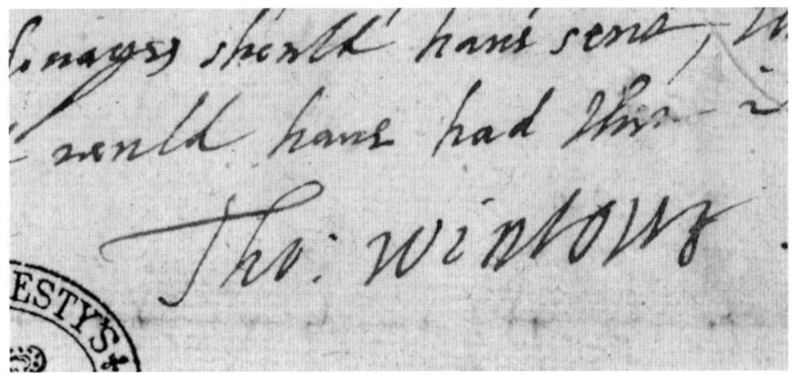

Thomas wintour's characteristic signature. On the fair copy of his confession (p.109), the name is written, not signed, and spelled 'Winter' (sp 14/216/117).

that Thomas Wintour was now sufficiently recovered from his injuries sustained at Holbeach to make a written confession.

Endless controversy has raged about the versions and authenticity of Thomas Wintour's confessions. The National Archives' copy, Sir Edward Coke's 'corrected' version of Wintour's confession, omits some of the human element from his account, distances Monteagle and makes Jesuit involvement explicit, but it agrees substantially with the original at Hatfield House. Unnecessary weight and argument has been attached to the fact that the date of The National Archives' version has been altered from the date the copy was made to the date of the original confession, and that the handwriting and 'signature' are quite obviously not Wintour's own. The use of fair copies of important evidence in legal cases, in absence of the photocopier, was perfectly standard in the period; they had been established as admissible in court following a precedent set by William Myll, Clerk of the Star Chamber, who had copied depositions taken in the High Court of Delegates for use in his own court in 1603. What is very nearly unforgeable about both the original confession and the copy is Wintour's literary style, the humorous rhythms and cadences of his prose and the naturalness of the dialogue, which historians have found so irresistible. Even after the attempts in official circles to make the plotters seem less human, something of the wit of his notes from the Low Countries remains in the style of the confession.

23–25 November 1605: Fair copy of Thomas Wintour's confession annotated by the king

Thomas Percy: The first word he spake (after he came into our company) was, Shall we always, gentlemen, talk and never do anything?

Robert Catesby: 'how necessary it was not to forsake our country … but to deliver her from out of the servitude where she remained.' 'To blow up the parliament house with gunpowder, for said he in that place have they done us all the mischief, and perchance God hath designed that place for their punishment.'

The fair copy of Thomas Wintour's confession, annotated by James between 23 and 25 November 1605. So much of the official version of events rests on Wintour's evidence that debate has raged about the confession's authenticity.

My most honorable Lords. 6

Not out of hope to obtayne pardon, for speakinge of my temporall part, I may say, the fault is greater then can be forgiven, nor affectinge hereby the title of a good subiect, for I must redeeme my countrey, from as great a danger, as I have hazarded the bringinge her into, before I can purchase any such opinion; Only at your Ho: command, I will briefly sett downe myne owne accusation, and how farr I have proceeded in this businesse, wch I shall the faythfuller doe, since I see such courses are not pleasinge to allmighty God, and that all, or the most materiall parts, have been allready confessed.

I remayned wth my brother in the countrey from Allhollantyde, untill the beginninge of Lent, [In the yeare of our Lord 1603 the first of the Kings Raigne] about wch tyme, Mr Catesby sent thither, entreatinge me to come to London, where he and other my friends would be glad to see me, I desired him to excuse me, for I founde not my selfe very well disposed, and (wch had happened never to me before) returned the messenger wthout my company, shortly I receaved an other lre, in any wise to come; at the second summons I presently came upp, and founde him wth Mr John Wright at Lambeth, where he brake wth me how necessarye it was not to forsake our countrey (for he knewe I had then a resolution to goe over) but to deliver her from the servitude, in wch she remayned, or at least to assist her wth our uttermost indevours, I answeared, that I had often hazarded my life upon farr lighter termes, and now would not refuse any good occasion, wherein I might doe service to the Catholicke cause, but for my selfe, I knew noe meanes probable to succeede, he sayde that he had bethought him of a way, at one instant to deliver us from all our bonds, and wthout any forrayne helpe to replant agayne the Catholicke religion, and wthall tould me in a word it was to blow upp the Parliamt howse wth gunpowder, for sayd he, in that place have they done us all the mischiefe, and perchance God hath designed that place for their punishmt.

Thomas Wintour 'wondered at the strangeness of the conceit' 'but if it should not take effect, as most of this nature miscarried, the scandal would be so great that Catholic religion might hereby sustain as not only our enemies butt our friends also would with good cause condemn us.'

To which Catesby replied 'The nature of the disease required so sharp a remedy.' (SP 14/216/114)

While Percy and Catesby had alternately boasted of their aristocratic connections and belittled their patrons for the ease with which they duped them, Thomas Wintour had a less extravagant, more pragmatic approach. He followed Lord Monteagle out of financial necessity, but spent little energy in protecting or implicating him. Likewise he served Spain to fill with pensions the gap in patronage left by the death of the Earl of Essex. He seems a much more reliable narrator. Though devout and committed to the plot, he did not react to the explosion at Holbeach so much as a sign of divine displeasure, rather as an accident of war, like the effect of the sea on the siege of Ostend. His reaction was practical, to fight to the last with the weapons available. Wintour, having furnished the authorities with much of what they needed to know of the plotters and their motivations, successfully established his own credibility. He went on to tell them rather more than they wanted to hear.

Thomas Wintour referred to communication with the plotters from Lord Monteagle in relation to their intrigues with Spain. Again he emphasized the importance of their rank in society. Monteagle's name was hastily scratched out and shamelessly pasted over.

25 November 1605: Wintour's tale – protecting Lord Monteagle

In the message that was delivered me from my [Lord Monteagle], Catesby and Tresham I was wished to say that those three were of a quality near connections, for if greater personages should have sent class of England would have had them in more suspicion. (SP 14/216/117)

The evidence of Francis Tresham, who admitted his desire to save Lord Monteagle from the intended explosion by covert means, 'to deliver myself from the infamous brand of an accuser and to save his life which in all true rules I was bound to do', also implicated Monteagle in the Spanish mission of Thomas Wintour. Monteagle's name was pasted out again.

A *Denies knowledge of planned invasion by Spanish forces.*
B *'Advised to bethink himself better', denies knowledge of Thomas Wintour's mission in Spain.*
C *Thought former questions were about James reign only, does remember Wintour's mission to Spain in 1602.*
D *Catesby and [Monteagle] knew of the mission*

(SP 14/216/117)

With the arrival of 'great men', such as Northumberland and Montagu in the Tower, Guy Fawkes found himself moved to lesser lodgings. This reflected the importance of social distinction even among prisoners, but also Fawkes's declining importance in the investigation. New lines of enquiry among the rich and powerful were opening up. And Sir William Waad, Lieutenant of the Tower,

Further evidence about the plot from Thomas Wintour, 25 November 1605. The original reference to Lord Monteagle in the opening line has been hastily pasted over as the authorities sought to distance him from the plot.

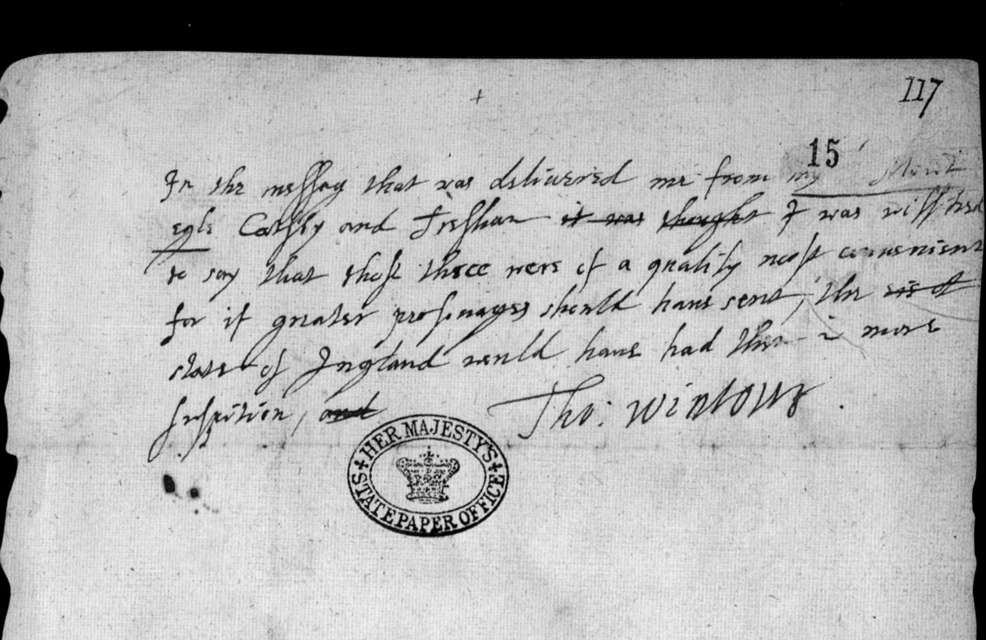

117

15

In the message that was delivered me from ~~my~~ [pasted over] Catesby and Tresham ~~it was thought~~ I was willed to say that those three were of a quality most convenient for if greater personages should have sent them the ~~rest of~~ state of England would have had them in more suspicion, ~~and~~

Tho: Wintour.

found himself running out of comfortable accommodation for all the lords being sent there. The prisoners of plots of 1603 would also have to make way.

Worse still for Fawkes, Coke had not let go of the passing reference to Sir Walter Raleigh in his early confessions. He planned on 25 November to harangue the prisoner on the subject of Sir Walter's connections with the plots of 1603 for which Raleigh had already been tried, convicted and, after a spectacular reprieve from execution, imprisoned in the Tower. 'Fawkes to be examined whether he heard not in Spain or elsewhere of the Lord Cobham's employment or any matter concerning Sir Walter Raleigh in that behalf.'

Coke was never one to let a present pressing treason get in the way of a two-year-old vendetta against some favourite foes. A professed traitor could become a reliable government witness in the pursuit of greater prey. It is perhaps indicative again of the danger of seeing the plot in purely ideological terms, that Raleigh, the great enemy of Catholic Spain, despite lack of evidence about any actual role in the plot, was suspected by the authorities – and the plotters themselves – as a likely man to support a Catholic coup d'état in England. Raleigh's thwarted ambition and reported dislike of his Scots king were quite enough to make him the focus of discontented parties of all convictions.

Ten days after dismissing the plot as a fable from the safety of Paris, Dudley Carleton was under arrest in Westminster. The fable became a grim reality as the amused social commentator became a suspect. The Earl of Northumberland wrote a letter supporting Carleton, 'formerly his secretary', but perhaps prudently did not send it. On 2 December 1605 Carleton wrote in a very different tone, pleading for his freedom to the Earl of Salisbury, after having been 'in restraint' for nine days.

> *From the bailiff's house in Westminster this 2nd December 1605*
> My Lord, I presume so much of your honourable favour that unless you thought I were well I would not lie by it this long and though for entreatment I have no cause to complain, yet I make so bold to write to your Lordship that I live in great misery. For there can be no greater burden to an honest mind than to be so long under suspicion of bearing part in so barbarous a villainy. Whereupon I beseech your Lordship and

> the rest of my most honourable lords that you will please to take some speedy course for your satisfaction in my behalf and whatsoever your justice shall assign me, I shall not complain of it. The greatest punishment shall be too little if the least fault can be proved against me and if nothing I hope your Lordships in your favourable judgements will think sufficient of nine days restraint as close prisoner and so I rest most humbly at your Lordship's disposal DC.

The note still displays the parallelisms and cleverness of his usual gossipy correspondence, but with considerable risk and strain. If the least offence really does merit the greatest punishment, he had certainly earned it by helping Thomas Percy obtain his lease.

Surviving letters show that Carleton was still suspected in the weeks that followed, and used the ingenious argument on 12 December that his continuing imprisonment was unfair since it made him look guilty. (He was still pleading to Salisbury at Christmas that he was 'a solitary prisoner at this merry time'.) Eventually Cecil did authorize his release, but as late as the end of February 1606 Carleton wrote to John Chamberlain from self-imposed exile, hoping to 'take away the scent of gunpowder' in the Chilterns and take advice on his further advancement from Sir Walter Cope, one of the lesser commissioners, to whom he had addressed pleading notes at Christmas. Once his gaoler, Cope had now become his host, and the narrow line between social acceptance and suspicion had been successfully negotiated.

On the same day as Carleton's pleading letter, Ambrose Rookwood was examined twice. His loss of social standing preoccupied him, too, his confessions reflecting on the quality of his horsemanship and horses and his loss of the latter. As Sir Everard Digby had done, Rookwood suggested that Catesby had been 'close' and not told the rich late recruits the whole truth, including the possibility of the plot's discovery. On Monday 4 November Catesby had employed him in buying 'necessaries', while Catesby and John Wright fled London without him. Thanks to his horses, he had been able to overtake them. Six days later Sir William Waad, in the same letter in which he revealed to Salisbury that 'John and Christopher Wright were schoolfellows of Fawkes and neighbours' children, Tesimond the Jesuit was at that time a schoolfellow also with them, so was this crew here all brought up together' also confirmed that Grant had four of the finest horses in the realm, and that Rookwood was still preoccupied with the fate of his animals.

The Daring of Digby

From this period comes our next image of Sir Everard Digby in his leading role, acting in a way in which none of the other surviving plotters would have dared. We must imagine his state of mind as he wrote, with all his erstwhile confidence, a letter to Salisbury offering his services as a diplomat between the king and the pope. It is one of the more remarkable and bizarre documents to come out of the plot. The letter is undated, but its social ease and assumption of bargaining power have so amazed historians that some have assumed it must come from the period before the discovery of the plot, before even Digby had joined the conspiracy. It is quite clear from the latter half of the letter, however, that Digby is writing in the full awareness that he has forfeited his life by what he calls 'our offence'. Again, the overriding sense we get from this neat, elegant, literate letter is Digby's idea of his own social standing and importance. The letter begins by recalling a conversation with Salisbury held months if not years before 'when his Majesty had done nothing against the Catholics' and aims to continue it as if nothing unpleasant has intervened. He has, it is true, been involved in a failed treason, but this should simply convince Salisbury that Catholic discontents are serious. Underneath this minor peccadillo he is still Sir Everard Digby, darling of the court, confidante of the most important English priests and the 'best sort' of English Catholics. Digby presents himself as the ideal man to represent the government he has just tried to destroy in negotiations with the papacy, to relieve the king from the threat of excommunication and reconcile him to his discontented Catholic subjects. Only he can secure the king's safety.

A LETTER from Sir Everard Digby to Salisbury, calendared December 1605. Even as a prisoner with no hope of reprieve, Digby offered to play a major role in negotiations between the king and the pope (transcription p.116).

course, to stop the efecte that may proceede from any discontented
or dispayringe Catholike.
and I doubt not but his returne would bringe you boath assurance
that such course should not be taken with the Kinge: and that it should be
performed agaynste any, that should seeke to disturbe him for religion.
if this were done there could then be no cause to feare any Catholike.
and this may be done only with those proceedings which as I understoode
yor Lo: should be used. if yor Lo: aprove it to be worth the doinge
I shalbe glad to be yor instrument. for no hope to put of from my
selfe any punishment: but only that I wishe saftie to the Kinge, and
ease to Catholike. if yor Lo: and the state thinke it fit to run another
course, and deale severely with Catholikes: give me leave to tell you
what I feare will hapen. which in breife wilbe massakers, rebelions,
and desperate attempts agaynste the Kinge and State.
for it is a generall receved reason amongst Catholikes, that there is
not that expectinge and sufferinge course now to be run, that was in
the Queenes time. who was the laste of her Line: and laste in expectance
to run violent courses agaynste Catholikes. for then was it hoped that
the Kinge that now is, would have bene at leaste free from persecuting,
as his promise was before his cominge into this Realme: and as
divers his promises have bene since his cominge: sayinge that he
would take no soule mony, nor blood: also as it apeared was the whole
bodie of the counsells pleasure, when they sent for divers of the beste
state of Catholikes, (as Sr Tho: Tresham and others) and tould them it was
the Kings pleasure to forgive the payment of Catholikes, so longe
as they should cary themselves dutifully and well. all these promises
every man sees broken. and to increase them further in dispayre,
moste Catholikes take note of a vehement booke written by Mr
Attorney, whose drifte (as I have heard) is to prove that the only
beinge a Catholike is to be a traytor. which booke cominge forth,
after the breach of so many promises, and before the endinge of
such a violent parlament: can worke no lesse efecte in mens
minde, then a beleefe that every Catholike wilbe brought within this
compasse, before the Kinge and State have done with them. and I knowe
as the preiste himselfe tould me, that if he had not hindered, there had
somewhat bene attempted before or offence, to give ease to Catholikes.

17

But beinge so easely prevented, and so necessarie to avoyde,
I doubt not but yor Lo: and the reste of the Lords will thinke
of a more milde and undoubted safe course. in which I will
undertake the performance of what I have promised and
as much as canbe expected. and when I have done
I shalbe as willinge to die, as I am ready to offer
my service. and expect not, nor desire favor for it,
either before the doinge it, or in the doinge it, or
after it is done. but refer my selfe to the resolved
course for me. so leavinge to trouble yor Lo: any
further I humbly take my leave.

Yor Lo:s poore bedesman.

The letter is, in fact, consistent with Digby's confessions. It is also perhaps not really so mistaken in contending what seems with hindsight to be incredible: that the government would view the plot, which had been stopped before it did much harm, as a minor infringement. Digby's letter is wild in places, but the report of his conversation with Salisbury on the dilemmas of Jacobean religious policy sounds genuine, and his attack on James's broken promises has been widely echoed.

December 1605[†]: Traitor and ambassador – Sir Everard Digby to the Earl of Salisbury

... If your Lordship apprehend it to be worth the doing I should be glad to be your instrument, from no hope to put off from myself any punishment, but only that I wish safety to the King and ease to Catholics. If your Lordship and the State think it fit to run another course and deal severely with Catholics, give me leave to tell you what I fear will happen, which in brief will be massacres, rebellions and desperate attempts against the King and state, for it is generally received reason among the Catholics that there is not that expecting and suffering course now to be run that was in the Queen's time who was the last of her line and last in expectance to run violent courses against Catholics. For it was hoped that the King that now is would have been at least free from persecuting as his promise was before coming into his realm and as divers his promises have been since his coming, saying that he would take no soul, money nor blood, which it appeared was the whole body of the Council's pleasure when they sent for divers of the best sort of Catholics (as Sir Thomas Tresham and others) and told them it was the King's pleasure to forgive the payment of Catholics so long as they should carry themselves dutifully and well. All these promises every man sees broken. And to thrust them further in despair more Catholics take note of a vehement book by Mr Attorney whose drift (as I have heard) is to prove that only to be a Catholic is to be a traitor, which book coming forth after the breach of so many promises and before the ending of such a violent parliament can work no less effect in men's minds than a belief that every Catholic will be brought within this compass before the King and state have done with them and I know, as the Priest himself told me, that if he had not hindered, there had somewhat been attempted before our offence to give ease to Catholics, but being easily prevented and so necessary to avoid, I doubt not but your Lordship and the rest of the lords will think of more a mild and

undoubted safe course in which I will undertake the performance of that I have promised and as much as can be expected and when I have done I shall be as willing to die as I am ready to offer my service and expect not nor desire favour for it, either before doing it, or in the doing it, or after it is done, but refer myself to the resolved course for me. So fearing to trouble your Lordship further, I humbly take my leave, your Lordship's poor beadsman Eve: Digby.

† calendared (SP 14/17/10)

Even at the last, there is very little humility. In offering himself as Salisbury's 'beadsman', Digby casts himself in role of a man of prayer whose efforts might ease Salisbury's soul. Essentially it is an assertion of the superiority and efficacy of his own religious belief. Having failed to put Salisbury in heaven with gunpowder, he offers to get him there in other ways. Unsurprisingly, however, Salisbury rejected Digby's offer.

Meanwhile, Digby's wife Mary was facing up to the financial consequences of her husband's treason and battling with zealous local authorities in Buckinghamshire who had stripped their house of possessions. She, too, wrote to Salisbury, more practically and with greater success than her husband had done, for relief from the depredations of the sheriff. Again it is perhaps an indication of the social standing of the Digbys that her claims were investigated and found support within the Exchequer and the Privy Council. The latter began the slow process of restoring her property to her.

The Yeoman's Tale

In less salubrious accommodation in the Tower, Thomas Bate, interrogated by a lesser commission of investigators, was less concerned with the loss of his property than of his life. Though Bate was a yeoman rather than a gentleman, he was a servant who possessed servants of his own, and a man of some importance in the organization of the Gunpowder Plot. He appears rather like one of the witty servants in a Shakespeare play, rather cleverer than his masters who are too wrapped up in their own preoccupations to see clearly. As Robert Catesby's confidential assistant, according to his own evidence, he guessed the nature of the plot, despite the efforts

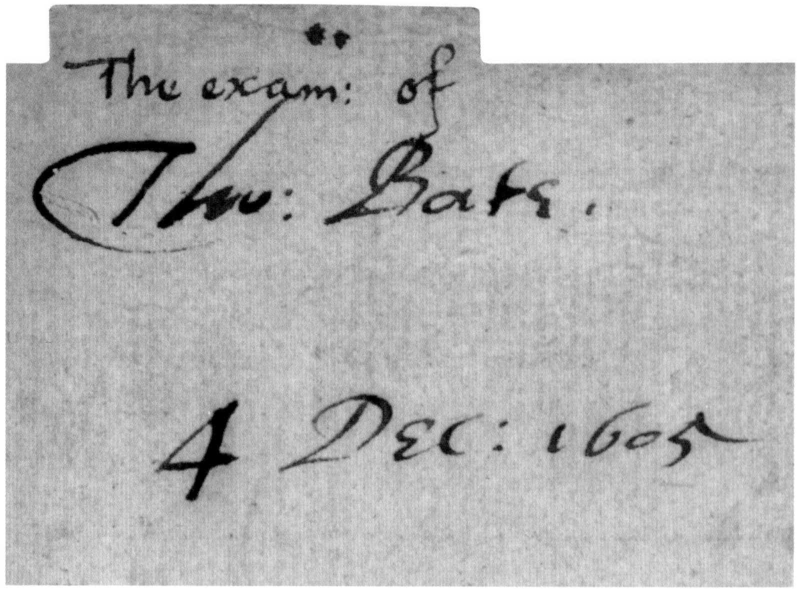

The exam: of
Tho: Bate.
4 Dec: 1605

THE EXAMINATION of Thomas Bate. As one of the 'lesser' prisoners Bate's confession was witnessed by investigators of lower rank, but his evidence was as literate as any of the gentlemen and betrayed a certain ironic wit (SP 14/216/145).

of the gentlemen to keep it secret. His educated guess necessitated his admission to the secret, and having thus earned the right to participate he presents himself in his evidence as a practical and determined man, drawn in by his social superiors but lacking their recklessness or ideology – cagier than the gentlemen who forfeit his life. Unlike Catesby, Bate was not full of philosophical justifications, but proud of his role and practical nous. Had it been left to me, he implies, there would have been less risk and a greater chance of success.

By the time Bate gave his own evidence the authorities had a good idea of his character and importance from the testimony of his wife Martha. She was examined on 8 November 1605, while he was still on the run after leaving the gentlemen to their suicidal last stand at Holbeach. She gave evidence that her husband left her on 5 November, taking five or six pistols with him, and ordered her to convey to Robert's mother Lady Catesby certain trunks of armour, which had lain there since the late queen's death. Bate himself gave evidence on 4 December that Catesby had sent him to look for lodgings 'near the Parliament house', a hint as to the nature of his master's business that he soon took up. Bate was no doubt keen to demonstrate the trust Catesby reposed in him and his own acumen in deducing what is going on, but this seems a bit amateurish: a top secret, treasonable mission entrusted to a third party not yet sworn to secrecy. In fact, the whole early stage of the plot as Bate describes it seems to be something of a game, buoyed by Catesby's presence and self-confidence – until the scene shifts suddenly to 6 November at Huddington, by which time they are all as good as dead. Even here there is an element of bravado: they had already hazarded their lives for less and the attempt was worth it. Nonetheless, Bate was not one to hang around when Catesby and John Wright suggested a poetic suicide pact at Holbeach using the remaining gunpowder.

4 December 1605: Thomas Bate's evidence

He confesseth that about this time twelvemonth his master asked this examinate, whether he could procure him a lodging near the Parliament House, he went to seek some such lodging and dealt with a baker that had a room joining to the Parliament House, but the baker answered that he could not spare it. After that (some fortnight or thereabouts as he thinketh) his master imagining as it seemed that this examinate suspected somewhat of that, that he, the said Catesby went about, called him to him at Puddle Wharf at the house of one Powell (where Catesby had taken a lodging) and in the presence of Thomas Wintour asked him 'what he thought what business they went about? And this examinate answered 'that he thought they went about some dangerous business' whereupon they asked him again, 'what he thought the business might be', and he answered that he thought they intended some dangerous matter about the Parliament House because he had been sent to get a lodging near that House. Whereupon they made this examinate take an oath to be secret in the business, which being taken to him, that it was true that they meant to do somewhat about the Parliament House, namely to lay powder under it to blow it up. Then they told him he was to receive the sacrament for the more assurance, and he thereupon went to confession to a priest named Greenway and in his confession told Greenway he was to conceal a very

B

Examination of Thomas Bates servant to Robert Catesby the 4th of Dec: 1605. before the lords Comissioners.

he confesseth that about this time twelvemonethes his mr. asked this exam.t whether he could procure him a lodging nere the parliament house, whereupon he went to seeke some such lodging and dealt with a baker that had a rome coming to the parliament house, but the baker answered that he could not spare yt.

After that (some fortnight or thereabouts as he thinketh) his mr imagining as yt seemed, that this exam.t suspected somewhat of that wch the said Catesby went about, called him to him at puddle wharffe in the house of one Powell (where Catesby had taken a lodging) and in the presence of Thomas winter, asked him what he thought, what busines they went about, and this exam.t answered that he thought they went about some dangerous busines, whereupon they asked him againe what he thought the busines might be And he answered that he thought they intended some dangerous matter about the parliament house, because he had ben sent to gett a lodging nere that house.

Thereupon they made this exam.t take an oath to be secrett in the busines, wch being taken by him, they told him that yt was true, that they ment to doe somewhat about the parliament house, namelye to lay powder under yt to blowe yt upp.

B Then they told him, that he was to receive the Sacrament for the more assurance, and he thereupon went to confession to a priest named Grenewaye, and in his confession told Grenewaye that he was to conceale a very dangerous peece of work, that his mr Catesby and Thomas winter had imparted unto him, and that he being fearfull of yt, asked the councell of Grenewaye, telling the said Grenewaye (wch he was not desirous to heare) their particular intent and purpose of blowing up the parliament house, and Grenewaye *dangerous piece of work that his master Catesby and Thomas Wintour had imparted unto him, and that he, being fearful of it, asked the counsel of Greenway, telling the said Greenway (which he was not desirous to hear) the particular purpose and intent of blowing up the Parliament House; and Greenway the Priest thereto said that he would take no notice thereof, but that he, the said examinate, should be secret in that his master imparted unto him, because it was for a good cause, and that he willed this examinate to tell no other Priest of it, saying moreover that it was not dangerous unto him, nor any offence to conceal it. And thereupon the said Priest Greenway gave this examinate absolution and he received the sacrament in the company of his master Robert Catesby and Thomas Wintour.*

He sayeth moreover that they were in consultation to send to Mr Talbot of Grafton to move him to go with them and to go unto him were named and appointed Sir Everard Digby, Stephen Littleton and Thomas Wintour, but Sir Everard Digby when he was going was stayed by the company and Stephen Littleton and Thomas Wintour only went. He sayeth also that they moved Robert Wintour to go, but he answered that he would not go, desiring to be excused for refusing, because he was in hope that Mr Talbot would be good to his wife and children.

Being asked whether he hath acquainted any other Priest with the conspiracy he sayeth no. But sayeth that he confessed himself to another Priest named Hammond, at Huddington, Robert Wintour's house, but that was only for his sins and not for any other particular cause. (SP 14/216/145)

Bate gives us another perspective on the scene at Huddington on 6 November. He is less careful than some of the 'gentlemen' of the reputation of the Jesuits, but he was also more likely to be ill treated by the authorities to gain incriminating evidence against them.

Dining with Danger

On 13 December, thanks to a chance conversation with a servant, Northumberland finally remembered what had happened when Percy had visited him for dinner on 4 November – the day before

Examination of Thomas Bate, 4 December 1605. Catesby could not keep the plot secret from a canny and observant servant (see transcription p.119).

the projected destruction of the Lords. Unlike lesser prisoners such as Thomas Bate, who were compelled to give evidence under threat of torture, Northumberland composed his own evidence and suggested to his fellow lords what they might make of it.

He began with a lengthy preamble on the nature of memory to explain his previous forgetfulness. Known to be deaf, his memory as well as his hearing could be as selective. As the earl describes it, Percy leads the conversation and possibly talks about him to his disadvantage below the level of the earl's hearing. If we had a mental picture of the quaking conspirator putting his head in the lion's mouth, risking a visit to his all-powerful patron in the hope of hearing some moment's conversation which might indicate that the plot was discovered, then the earl's version of events forces us to think again. If anything, Percy is the man with the power and information; the earl trails rather in his wake. Here is a glimpse of the manipulator and embezzler who used the earl's position to gain access to the royal family, but was apparently prepared to see him die with them.

13 December 1605: Dinner at Syon House

As we sat at dinner, Percy asked Sir William Lower 'What news of the Parliament?' who answered, None that he heard of; with that Percy draws out a little paper, wherein [*were*] *the sum of the articles agreed by the commissioners, which were nine as I remember, saying 'We have more in the North than you have here'. They looking upon these articles, I asked what they were; they showed them me; I read them; upon speech how I defend them upon examination your lordships may know; what they said one to another I know not, but as much as I heard was not material, nor do I speak it for that, but as an argument wherefore Percy came thither that day (not to discover anything more), how probable this is, that, that was put out for a bait, whether I understood any thing of the Lord Monteagle's letter; and this does not greatly disagree from that your lordships said, that Percy to some of his companions said, I will to Syon, and then I will tell you more; for it is to be supposed, that either*

Northumberland's evidence to the Lords Commissioners, 13 December 1605. The earl's account of his dinner with Thomas Percy on the eve of the plot's discovery seems to confirm Percy's private boasting of his ability to deceive his master.

My Lords; As your Lordps: intergatories are generall for the most, soe can it not chuse but the memory ~~for the~~ of man must be forgettfull in the perticulars vnexprest yett infolded in thos ge=nerallytes.

To one intergatory last demanded I answered negatiuely as my remembrance then serued me; and it is the 6 as I take it; singe tyme and a thinking prisoner hathe begott that whiche an euell memory had laid to rest, a thing forgotten out of memory, not out of will as shall appere, for it must nedes ~~soe~~ yelde somme kind of satisfaction to your Lordps: in the mane point of all: And I know your Lordps; are all soe charitable that yow had rather

C fynde me an honest man to the state then falty to my King.

The intergatory was this: what discours of matter of importance was at my table the munday the 4 of Nouember.

My answer was noen, as far as I did remember.

D Since whiche tyme a poore man of myne that waites of me in my chamber by way of other talke made me remember that as we satt at dinner, Percy asked Sir William Lower what newes of the Parlement, whoe answered noen that he herd of; with that Percy drawes out a littell paper wherein the summe of the articles agreed of by the commissioners, whiche were 5 as I remember, saing we haue more in the north then yow haue here. They looking vpon theas articles I asked what they were; they shewed them me; I red them, vpon speche how I defend them vpon examination your Lordps may know; what they said one to an other I know not but as mutche as I herd was not materiall, nether dos I speake it for that, but as an argument wherefore ~~came~~ Percy came thither that day, (not to giue me warning but to haue somme light and whether he could discouer any thing or noe) how probable this is, that, that was put out for a bate whether I vnderstood any thing of the Lord Moteagles Letter; and this doeth not mutche disagre from that your Lordps said, that Percy to somme of his compagnons said I will to Syon, and then I will tell yow more; for it is to be supposed, that ether out of my Lord of Montegles acquaintance with me, or out of being a priuy counsellor I must vnderstand somwhat if things were discouered, and yett durst he not aske wether there were any thing or noe. Now your Lordps: knowes this circumstance, I refferre it to your wisdoms what construction to make of it and whether if I had bene warned, sutche a stale had not bene better in priuat then at dinner. Thus recommending this and all the rest to your honorable censurs I rest

Your Lordps: to doe yow seruis

Northumberland

This 13 December.

out of my Lord Monteagle's acquaintance with me, or out of being a Privy Councillor, I must understand somewhat if things were discovered and yet durst he not ask whether there were anything or no. Now your lordships knoweth this circumstance I refer it to your wisdoms what construction to make of it and whether if I had been warned, such a tale had not been better in private than at dinner. Thus recommending this and all the rest to your honourable censures I rest your lordships: to do you service, Northumberland.

(SP 14/17/39)

Sir William Lower had already been examined on this conversation on 2 December. He remembered even less, even whether Thomas Hariot (the astronomer and mathematician, patronized by both Walter Raleigh and Northumberland, and thus also briefly a suspect in the plot) was present or not, perhaps believing nothing he said could do him any good. Anti-Scots as well as anti-Protestant feeling is clearly preying on Percy's mind on 4 November – the mischief of Parliament in (apparently) moving towards a Union of England and Scotland rather than simply its anti-Catholic legislation.

The earl was questioned repeatedly about his conduct towards Thomas Percy and the trust reposed in him, and his answers sounded

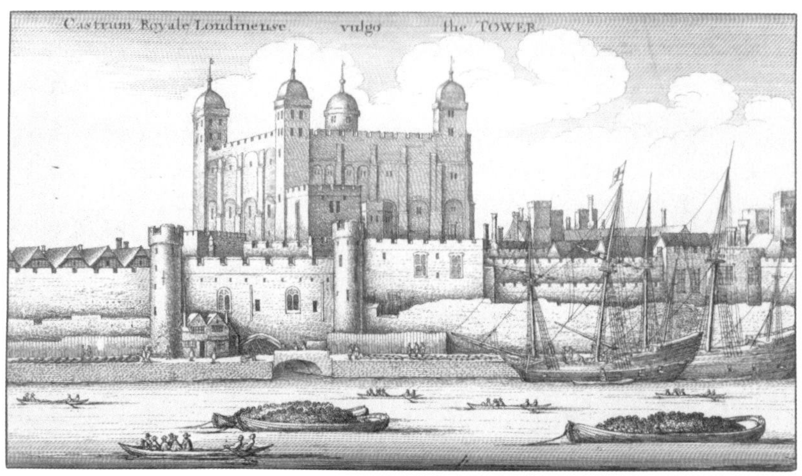

AN ENGRAVING of the Tower of London by Wenceslaus Hollar, 1647. The Tower was far from being a sterile dungeon; life flowed on inside and out, and the Earl of Northumberland lived in some splendour there.

unconvincing and contradictory. He thought Percy had taken the oath of allegiance though he had not administered it; he wrote to Percy only to keep track of him, as he did not entirely trust him. But if he did not trust him why make him a gentleman pensioner and put him so close to the king? Perhaps only James and Northumberland knew how close Percy had come to the king and the murderous opportunities he might have had among the cloak-and-dagger negotiations 'in the owl-light' before James's accession in 1603.

Death in Darkness

In the dark night of a chamber in the Tower, Francis Tresham finally succumbed to illness in a state of physical agony and moral and spiritual confusion.The main preoccupation of his keeper Sir William Waad, apart from the disposal of the diseased corpse, was the social standing of the man and his powerful friends who seemed confident of his acquittal had he been tried for his part in the plot.

23 DECEMBER 1605: WAAD REPORTS TRESHAM'S DEATH IN THE TOWER (2 AM)

As I certified to your lordship there was no hope of recovery in Tresham, so it will please you to understand that he died this night, about two of the clock after midnight, with very great pain; for though his spirits were much spent, and his body dead, a-lay above two hours in departing. It may please your Lordship; I may know his Majesty's pleasure for the burying of him, both because it will not be possible to keep him, for he smelt exceedingly when I was with him yesterday in the afternoon, and I perceive means will be made to his Majesty, to have his body begged, for I find his friends were marvellous confident, if he had escaped this sickness, and have delivered out words in this place that they feared not the course of justice. So expecting what direction I shall follow, I commit your lordship to God's protection, this Monday the 23rd of December 1605. (SP 14/17/56)

Tresham's prominence as a man of considerable landed estates created a legacy of difficulties for the authorities. He died unconvicted of any offence, and the evidence against him was no more – or perhaps no less – strong than that against Lord Monteagle. The

As I certified your lo:p there was no hope of recovery in Tresham
so it will please you to understand that he died this night about
two of the clock after midnight wth very great payne, for though
his spirits were much spent, and his body dead, a lay about two
howers in departing. It may please your ho: lo:p I may
know his ma:tes pleasure for the burying of him both because
it will not be possible to keep him for his smell exceedingly
when I was wth him yesterday in the afternoone and 75
I perceive meanes wilbe made to his ma:tie to have his
body begged, for I find his frinds were marvelous
confident if he had escaped this sicknes, and have delivered
out words in this place that they feared not the course of
Justice, So expecting what direction I shall follow I
comitt your lo:p to gods protection this munday the 23 of
December 1605.

Humblie at the Comaundement of your ho: lo:p

W. Waad

government had lengthy trouble in having his goods and lands confiscated as a traitor because he had never been indicted. The House of Commons, for all its initial elation and desire for justice against the plotters of its destruction, was reluctant to undo the conventions on which the power of its members rested. If Tresham, recent head of a prominent Northamptonshire family, might forfeit his property merely on suspicion, what precedent might this set for the MPs themselves? It would later emerge that Tresham had dictated a deathbed retraction of his previous evidence, and had owned and read a Jesuit treatise on equivocation. But was the evidence or the retraction the equivocation? Perhaps only one man knew, the man who became the new prime suspect for the authorities and who, unknown to them, had written the treatise, Father Henry Garnet.

The authorities took a relaxed Christmas break from the investigation of the plot, giving a chance for the Jesuits to flee the country and spare the government the political embarrassment of their martyrdom. In the New Year, final attempts began to force the plotters to confess some international involvement, preferably the papacy rather than Spain. They began to concentrate their efforts on emphasizing the role of Father Henry Garnet in an attempt to prove loyal English Catholics had been led into treachery by theological sophistry. Developments in January brought fresh reports of the dishevelled and abandoned state of the plotters after Holbeach, which rather undermined attempts to prove any high-powered aristocratic patronage of their cause. The long-awaited trial and execution of the plotters coincided with the betrayal of Garnet's hiding place and, after more than a week of searching, his apprehension in a priest's hole at Hindlip House.

While Garnet hid, Robert Wintour was finally captured. He had been on the run for two months after fleeing from Holbeach early on 8 November, hiding with Stephen Littleton, the owner of Holbeach, in 'barns and poor men's houses' across Worcestershire, before being betrayed to the authorities at Hagley. William

William Waad's report of Francis Tresham's death, 23 December 1605. Waad feared that the member of a prominent county family would have sufficient 'friends' to oppose legal moves against him and his estates (see transcription p.125).

Whorwood, the new Sheriff of Worcestershire (Sir Richard Walsh had been censured and removed for his precipitate actions after the dissent among the law officers as to the conduct of the siege at Holbeach), reported the arrest of Wintour and Littleton. A proclamation had been issued for Wintour's capture on 18 November, but he remained at large until 9 January 1606.

In the weeks between his capture and execution, Wintour confided to Guy Fawkes that while he was on the run he was troubled by recurrent dreams in which he saw the faces of those burned by the gunpowder explosion at Holbeach. He had first had this dream on 4 November, the day before the planned explosion in Parliament, but he later recognized in it images not of their intended victims, but of themselves. Wintour also reported 'a strange dream he had in the country that he thought he was in Cheapside, and looking towards [St] Pauls, it was all coated black and the stones were ready to fall'. His dream and the conversation in the Tower with Guy Fawkes were recorded by eavesdroppers and re-told at their trial to show them unrepentant, Fawkes confirming that Wintour 'saw the steeples of St Paul's and other churches stand awry and in one of the churches (it being now some church) he saw strange faces'. In reality, Wintour's dream, like all dreams, could be interpreted in a number of ways. Was it an indication of intended revolution within the church or of divine displeasure at the plot, signalled by the gunpowder explosion at Holbeach?

Despite Robert's efforts not to involve him, Sir John Talbot was ordered to London – 'setting aside all excuses' – for questioning after his son-in-law's capture. The authorities still groped for more aristocratic connections for the plotters – a noble mastermind to oversee a coup of a type they would understand. The link between Robert Wintour and the Earl and Countess of Shrewsbury yielded little, but it was still to prove useful for the conspirator. As he had wished, the family later did what it could to protect his wife and children after his death.

Robert Wintour was also questioned at length. Interestingly, he was asked whether Monteagle had 'begged of' the conspirators, which historians have taken to mean that Monteagle may have asked for pardons for them. It seems more likely that this question arose from the discovery of Monteagle's debts to Thomas Percy and, as Thomas Wintour confirmed, in fact Monteagle had borrowed money from other plotters too. For passing on the warning, Monteagle received public praise, lands worth £200 a year and an annual pension of £500.

On 15 January 1606 the government issued more 'Wanted!' descriptions, this time for the priests Henry Garnet and Oswald Tesimond. Garnet was described as:

> of a middling Stature, full Faced, Fat of body, of Complexion fair: his Forehead high on each side, with a little thin Haire coming down upon the middest of the forepart of his Head: the Hair of his Head and Beard grizzled: of Age between fifty and threescore: his Beard on his Cheeks cut close, on his Chin but thin, and somewhat short: his Gate upright, and comely for a Fat man.

The description of January 1606 gives a clear picture of Tesimond, not just of his features but also of his fashionable Italian clothes. The government regarded these as tools in the Jesuit's armoury, luring fashionable young men to conversion with the continental sophistication which the Catholic world afforded:

15 January 1606: A description of Oswald Tesimond

Of a reasonable stature, black hair, a brown beard cut close on the cheeks and left broad on the chin, somewhat long-visaged, lean in the face but of a good red complexion, his nose somewhat long and sharp at the end, his hands slender and long fingers, his body slender, his legs of a good proportion, his feet somewhat long and slender. His apparel of cloth, hose and jerkin much after the Italian fashion, the jerkin buttoned on the breast, his cloak buttoned down before with ribbands hanging down on his breast, his hat narrow-brimmed with a small band and broad full crown as now the fashion is. (SP 14/18/21)

Tesimond later came to the anonymity of London and saw, in the best thriller tradition, someone reading the proclamation against him and eyeing him intently. Successfully fending off an attempt by a pursuivant to arrest him in London, he holed up in Catholic houses in Essex and Suffolk until he was able to take a small boat to Calais with a cargo of dead pigs, of which he passed as the owner. After some time at St Omer, he moved south. In a letter to James I

of a resonable stature, blacke hayre
a browne bearde close cut on the cheekes
and lefte broade on the chine somwhat
longe visaged leane in the face but of a
good red complexione his nose somwhat
longe and sharpe at the ende his handes
slender and longe fingers his body slender
his legs of a good proportion his feete some-
thinge longe and slender
his aparell of clothe hose and jerkine much
after the Italyan fashione the jerkine buttoned
on the breste his cloake buttoned downe
before with ribandes hanginge downe
on his breste his hatt narow brimde
with a smal bande and a broad full
crowne as now the fashion is

of 1610, Sir Edwin Rich reported Tesimond's arrival in Naples, warning the king of a still greater threat posed by Tesimond's Italian fashion – a gift of poisoned clothing which the priest was supposed to be sending him.

Eight plotters – Guy Fawkes, Thomas and Robert Wintour, Robert Keyes, John Grant, Thomas Bate, Ambrose Rookwood and Sir Everard Digby – were finally tried in Westminster Hall on 27 January 1606. Digby, whose treason was first committed in a different county to the others, was tried upon a separate indictment at the end of the day; alone among the eight accused, he pleaded guilty. This gave him the opportunity to make a speech with the stage to himself. Digby repeated the assertion made in his letter to Salisbury, that the king had reneged upon promises of toleration for Catholics, and claimed that his affection for Catesby and desire to ease the lot of Catholics had prompted his actions. He knew, as he had known when he wrote his letter to Salisbury, that he could not hope to alter 'the resolved course for him', but his manner and bearing impressed many in the packed hall. After the verdict, of the eight accused only Digby spoke. He addressed the assembled lords: 'If I may but hear any of your lordships say you forgive me I shall go more cheerfully to the gallows.' Again, he believed his personality might move the intended victims of the explosion to

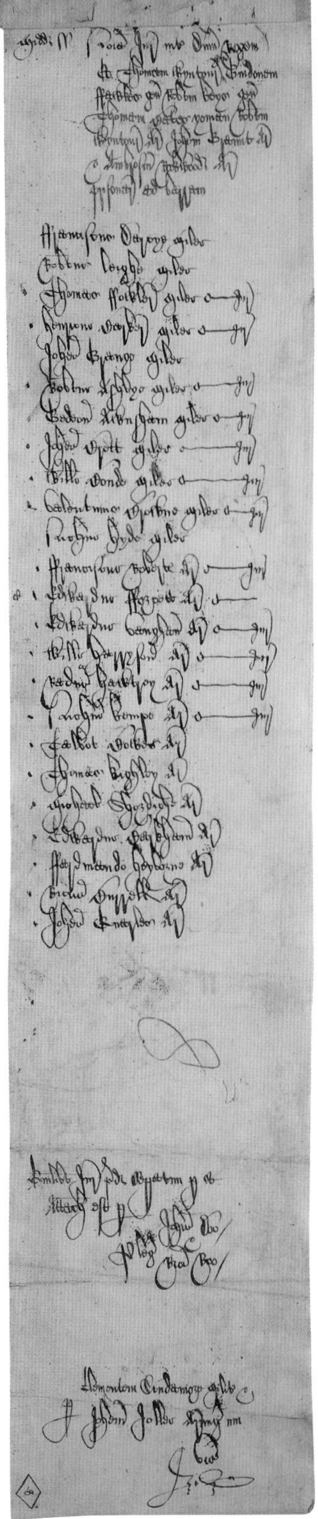

A DESCRIPTION of Oswald Tesimond (left), 15 January 1606. His Italian style of clothing, like Thomas Wintour's Italian books, showed affinity with the Catholic world beyond England's shores (see transcription p.129). The imposing documents (right) in special oyer and terminer roll and file recording the plotters' trial (KB 8/59).

treat him differently. To some extent he was right, for he received the gentle, ambiguous reply 'God forgive you and we do'. After being found guilty, Robert Wintour confined himself to a simple plea for mercy, while Thomas 'only desired that he might be hanged both for his brother and himself'. Fawkes justified his not guilty plea on the grounds that the indictment was inaccurate, exaggerating the role of the Jesuits.

On 30 January Digby and his co-conspirators Robert Wintour, John Grant and Thomas Bate were drawn on traitors' hurdles through streets to St Paul's churchyard, where a gallows had been erected. All four were drawn and quartered after only a brief hanging, to ensure they were still alive as they were dissected. The first to suffer, Digby met his death bravely. His biographer John Aubrey, with his usual ear for a good story, claimed that Digby's character and sense of the dramatic survived his execution: 'When his heart was plucked out by the Executioner (who cried … "Here is the

AN ENGRAVING of 1606 showing the plotters being brought to execution. Their deaths were carefully managed spectacles of exemplary punishment, but bravery and a well-turned speech could still win sympathy from the crowd.

heart of a Traitor!"), it is credibly reported he replied, "Thou liest!"'

Robert Wintour also had an eye on posterity, according to other remarks reported from his conversation with Guy Fawkes in the Tower. Defiantly, he suggested that their deaths would be followed by others in an unending struggle: 'God will raise up seed to Abraham out of the very stones, our deaths shall be sufficient justification of it. And it is for God's cause.'

After his death, new insight into Robert Wintour's activities and dilemmas in the days before the discovery of the plot emerged from the shadows. Two sets of Exchequer depositions, dating from 1608–9, illustrate how Sir Thomas Overbury, whose murder was at the centre of one the great Jacobean court scandals, haggled with Robert Wintour's widow over Robert's rights to salt deposits in Droitwich. The cases take evidence from 'Leonard Smallpeece, 54, of Pepper Hill, Salop', Sir John Talbot's steward, to whom Wintour wrote his desperate note from Huddington on 6 November. Smallpeece and other witnesses attest to Sir John Talbot's business dealings with the Wintours and John Grant immediately before 5 November. Wintour's dealings with his father-in-law seem nervous even then, and his actions were not conspicuously those of a man about to risk his position and his life in 'open rebellion'.

On 3 November, the Sunday evening before the plot was discovered, Wintour was transacting business at Grafton. He signed indentures making over his rights to the salt deposits; they needed to be sealed to make the contract binding, but Wintour was willing to postpone sealing the indentures until the following Saturday (9 November) rather than risk his father-in-law's annoyance by getting him out of bed late. If he was drawing up the indentures to secure the salt rights in his family should his personal property became forfeit (as it would if and when the plot was discovered), his readiness to delay seems hard to understand. Perhaps his urgency would be impossible to explain without hinting too heavily that something major was planned. Perhaps Wintour was consistent in being more fearful of his father-in-law than he was of the wildness of Robert Catesby. The result is not in doubt: the indentures were never sealed.

On 29 January 1606, the day before the first tranche of conspirators were dispatched, the poet and courtier Sir Arthur Gorges had reported warily on the impropriety of using St Paul's as a place of execution for the conspirators. In doing so, he betrayed fear of implicating himself in any criticism of the government line – 'but I willingly submit my opinion to your wisdom' – yet was also convinced of the possible political damage in feeding Catholic 'calumny' of Protestants as defilers of holy places. Perhaps his words had their effect, because the second set of executions on 31 January took place in the Old Palace Yard, Westminster. Parliamentary justice and poetic justice replaced divine retribution. There, to echo Catesby's words, they would have done all the mischief. Here Thomas Wintour, Ambrose Rookwood, Robert Keyes and Guy Fawkes suffered the same fate as their friends. Fawkes was the last of the eight to die.

The search for Henry Garnet at Hindlip House had begun on 20 January. He and Edward Oldcorne were finally discovered on 27 January, the day of the plotters' trial, but only on the day of the first executions did the government receive a full account of Garnet's arrest. Again, there is a nice mix of private and public interest in the man leading the search, Sir Henry Bromley, who found his duty dovetailed nicely with an opportunity to acquire land adjoining his own. If Fawkes had provided the vital if reluctant source of information in the first act, Thomas Wintour was the better, perhaps too well, informed source for the second. In Father Henry Garnet, the government now had a leading man for the third act, whose cleverness and social standing were to cause them even more trouble than the others.

Act III : *In Hiding and In the Wings*

FEBRUARY TO JUNE 1606

CAST LIST

Henry Percy, Earl of Northumberland, captain of the king's bodyguard, 'The Wizard Earl'

Henry Howard, Earl of Northampton, Privy Councillor 'Conjuror of priests and devils'

Robert Cecil, Earl of Salisbury, Principal Secretary of State, 'The Little Beagle'

William Parker, Lord Monteagle, defender of Catholics in Parliament, recipient of 'The Monteagle Letter'

Anthony Maria Browne, Lord Montagu, nobleman, employer of Guido Fawkes

Sir Edward Coke, Attorney General, prosecutor and conspiracist

Sir Thomas Edmondes, English Ambassador in Flanders

Henry Garnet, alias Walley, alias Farmer, alias Darcy, Father Superior of the English Jesuit Province

Oswald Tesimond, alias Greenway, alias Greenwell, missionary priest, schoolfellow of Guido Fawkes

Edward Oldcorne, alias Hall, missionary priest, schoolfellow of Guido Fawkes

Nicholas Owen, servant to Henry Garnet, carpenter and saint

Thomas Phelippes, correspondent of exiled Catholics, forger

Anne Vaux, 'virtuous Catholic gentlewoman'

Diplomats, priests and poets
Pursuivants, agents and informers
Staunch countrymen

The Great and the Good

By dramatic convention the plotters' trial should have been the end of the action: sentences handed out with poetic justice and loose ends conveniently tied up. In reality, things were not so simple. The Attorney General Sir Edward Coke spent the trial hinting that the eight being tried were simply the actors in the plot. The director, the criminal mastermind, he implied, had yet to be found. Despite all the evidence that Catesby had been the prime mover, experience of previous plots made the government very reluctant to believe that there was no such hidden figure. Yet each had their own preferences for the role. Sir Edward Coke picked up on passing references in Fawkes's confessions and identified Sir Walter Raleigh as plotting while imprisoned in the Tower. The Earl of Salisbury favoured troublesome Englishmen abroad, such as Hugh Owen, the English intelligencer at the imperial court in Brussels, or the Jesuits, and there is some evidence that part of his motivation was to absolve English Catholics of any native treason and blame foreign influence. Viewed as a whole, the effect of Salisbury's agenda on the investigation of the plot and the presentation of the evidence was significant but not sinister, and its objects, though not publicly stated, are clear from the documents. Strenuous efforts began to establish a Jesuit connection and the hand of dissident Englishmen abroad, to discover whether any 'great man', especially Northumberland, was involved and to distance Lord Monteagle from the plot. There was also some political capital to be made in blaming individuals whom the authorities had no realistic chance of catching, so that the sinister threat to the new-found stability of James's dynasty remained, a constant reminder of the government's great escape.

The Earl of Northampton had contributed to the theatricality of the plotters' trial. He exercised his natural talent for long, learned speeches, scorning the social standing of the plotters and dwelling on the presumption of over-mighty subjects in daring to rebel – the implication perhaps being that only nobility such as his own family, the Howards, should be allowed to do it. However, in Henry Garnet, Father Superior of the English Jesuit Province, the government now had the perfect material to test the hypothesis of the missing organizing genius to breaking point. They also had the Earl of Northumberland, imprisoned in the Tower since the end of November but as yet untried. Neither line of enquiry was to prove particularly comfortable for the government. In Henry Garnet's case, Salisbury was faced with the potential embarrassment of Jesuit martyrdom and the diplomatic awkwardness of uncovering past invasion plots by King James's valuable new ally, Spain. In Northumberland's case there was the prospect, hardly welcome to the king, of discovering support for the plot among the nobility he had done so much to rehabilitate and create as his own network of patronage in England.

Wary of what their continuing investigations might reveal, Salisbury found these had taken on a momentum of their own. Sir Edward Coke had no misgivings about uncovering aristocratic conspiracy. He contrived to forget royal instructions and conspicuously failed to exonerate Lord Monteagle. If Monteagle had not received the warning letter, apparently through the happy accident of being Francis Tresham's brother-in-law, there is little doubt that there was enough evidence, in the event hastily suppressed, to implicate him heavily in past plots and the plotters' circle, if not in the Gunpowder Plot itself. Worse consequences might have ensued than for the lords Stourton, Mordaunt and Montagu, whose connections with the plotters were more distant. Instead of land and financial reward, Monteagle might have found himself in Stourton's position, pleading to Salisbury for his liberty in August 1606.

Coke had also fastened on the circumstantial evidence against the Earl of Northumberland. His pedigree made him uniquely suitable as a lord protector sympathetic to Catholics; and he had appointed Percy to the king's bodyguard without ensuring he had taken the oath. Furthermore, Northumberland had sent enquiries to the North about his estate rents on 5 November without ordering the apprehension of Thomas Percy, responsible for their collection. In the Percy's structure of patronage, Northumberland was answerable for his cousin and, as accusations concerning the unravelling plot were rampant, it seems strange that he failed to mention Thomas as a prime suspect in the plot. The 'Wizard Earl' also had a

SIR ROBERT CECIL, Earl of Salisbury, from the studio of John de Critz. Cecil often doubted the value of those employed in his intelligence network, and the quality of information they supplied.

love of arcane experiment and a rumoured association with the dark arts; he was also interested in using astrology to predict the king's lifespan. The earl also maintained a friendship with Sir Walter Raleigh, suspicious in Coke's eyes. There were rumours that Percy had warned Northumberland at the Syon House dinner on 4 November, and that Northumberland, like Monteagle, had received a warning letter, but, unlike Monteagle, had concealed it. In his defence against such rumours, Northumberland disclosed that Percy, far from wishing to preserve him, treated him with contempt and 'railed' against him – behaviour based on an idea, however misplaced, of his social superiority, revealed when Percy 'pretended himself to be of the elder house … which showed he thirsted after the earldom'.

Secrets and Lies

The government also struggled to exploit what political capital there was to be made from the plot's discovery. There were allegations as early as November 1605 that Salisbury himself had devised the Gunpowder Plot to elevate his own importance in the eyes of the king, and to facilitate a further attack on the Jesuits. There were also constant reports suggesting that stopping the plot had not stopped plotting – on the contrary, it fostered a climate of suspicion in which anything seemed possible. The Gunpowder Plot could not be viewed in isolation, but was part of a series of possible conspiracies from known malcontents.

If ever we are tempted to view the Gunpowder Plot, and the investigation which followed, as unique events peculiar in their methods, a quick look at the career of Thomas Phelippes makes it clear that the gathering of secret intelligence – and indeed the manufacturing of documents – was a full-time industry. It was maintained by a select band of spies, forgers and decipherers, employed by the state but dangerous to the establishment by their very knowledge. The murky world of the Gunpowder Plot is made very much murkier thanks to men such as Phelippes. They spent half their time forging, deciphering and gathering intelligence for the government and the other half being suspected of complicity in the plots

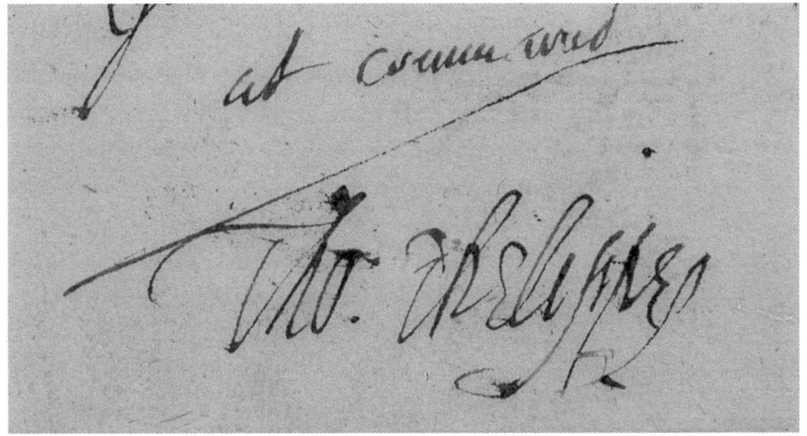

The signature of Thomas Phelippes (detail from SP 14/18/61). After a career forging the writing of others for the state, Phelippes found his own letters the subject of close scrutiny.

they were paid to uncover. If nothing else, Phelippes shows the limits of the trust Salisbury placed in intelligence and the pitfalls of gathering it.

Heavily implicated in the concoctions of the Babington Plot which brought down Mary Queen of Scots, Phelippes was never likely to prosper under the rule of her son, James I. He, unsurprisingly, was neglected, and when the state did have need of him, found himself working always in arrears in paying off his debt to the crown for his part in Mary's death. When it appeared that Phelippes had corresponded with Hugh Owen, continuing to do so after Guy Fawkes had revealed that Owen was the means by which the plot was to be justified on the continent after the explosion, his fortunes plunged to a still lower ebb. This is not to say that he was no longer useful, and fierce controversy has raged about the documents in which he might have had a hand, from the Monteagle letter itself to Henry Garnet's letters to Anne Vaux.

The government suspected Phelippes of duplicity in his dealings with Hugh Owen long before the discovery of the Gunpowder Plot. In January 1605 John Chamberlain reported 'I heard yesterday that Phillips the decipherer was apprehended and committed with all his

It may please your Lo. tho I have great cause to be greved
that your Lo. sholde hold any suspicion of me yett I am content
to be tryed hoping yt though my ennemy will not leave to
calumniate your Lo. will leave in the ende to thinke ill of me
Sr Tho. Fowlar hath surveyed all my writings wch were once
under sealey as your Lo. knowes afore and returned back your Lo. having still
my trunke wth all state causes. I leave to his owne report
how curiously he hath observed your Lo. warrant breaking
upp for his discharge all my wifes cabinetts and trunkes
whereof the keys were not left by her being these 9. months
out of towne. I am only in particular to satisfy
your Lo. of one thing: wch is that Barnes at his going
over the last weke prayed me he might for safety his owne
lodging being ~~but~~ in a commen place, leave a certen male of
apparell wch he brought over from the other side for one of
the Sp. Emb. servants wch I never so much as loked into
but it seems there were certen letters also for that party
wch Mr Fowlar hath and I hope have nothing of moment
For I know Barnes to be ~~an~~ honestly desposed to do your
Lo. service. And so I leave my self to your L.
honorable care and comend God preserve.

Your Lo. most humble
at commaund

Tho. Phelippes

papers seized.' With the discovery of the plot the arch-forger, decipherer and intelligence gatherer found that his own letters to Hugh Owen, designed to draw the recipient into confessing his knowledge of the plot, were being transcribed and sent to Salisbury's secretary as evidence of his own involvement. The scales tipped more heavily against Phelippes in January 1606, with Guy Fawkes's admission of Hugh Owen's role in the plot and the revelation of Phelippes's continued correspondence with him.

UNDATED LETTER, FEBRUARY 1606: A FORGER SUSPECTED – THOMAS PHELLIPES TO THE EARL OF SALISBURY

It may please your Lordship [*that*] *though I have great cause to be grieved that your Lordship should hold any suspicion of me, yet I am content to be tried, hoping that though my enemy will not leave to calumnate, your Lordship will leave in the end to think ill of me. Sir Thomas Fowler hath surveyed all my writings, which were once under survey before, as your Lordship knoweth, and returned back, your Lordship having still my trunk with all state causes. I leave to his report how curiously he hath observed your Lordship's warrant, breaking up for his discharge, all my wife's cabinets and trunks, whereof the keys were not left by her being these nine months out of town. I am only in particular to satisfy your Lordship of one thing; which is that Barnes at his going over the last week prayed me he might for safety, his own lodging being a common place, leave a certain make of apparel which he brought over from the other side, for one of the Spanish Ambassador's servants, which I never so much as looked into, but it seems there were certain letters also for the party, which Mr Fowler hath and I hope nothing of moment, for I know Barnes to be honestly devoted to do your Lordship's service. And so I leave myself to your Lordship's honourable carriage, whom God preserve, your Lordship's most humble at command Tho: Phellipes.* (SP 14/18/61)

This letter earned Phelippes a chance to explain himself to Salisbury in person, but the meeting did not go well. When Phelippes wrote once more on 4 February 1606, his stock had fallen still further.

THOMAS PHELIPPES's letter to the Earl of Salisbury, February 1606. Phelippes was so immersed in the affairs of state and the espionage business that his protestations of innocence were greeted with scepticism.

Unfortunately for him, all his secret undertakings with Spanish agents – many of whom could themselves have been double agents – could be interpreted in many ways. Salisbury's secretary has underlined passages in his next letter in which Phelippes recalls hearing of 'Catesby's insurrection' from a Catholic whose brother was in service with the Countess of Arundel. Perhaps here was another connection between the gentlemen's plot and 'the great'. Another school of thought would suggest this correspondence between Salisbury and the forger, coming as it did between Garnet's apprehension and his arrival in London, is just too neat a coincidence. Could Phelippes have been brought in by the government on a trumped-up charge to forge Garnet's letters?

The extent to which Phelippes's work in relation to the plot could be said to have repaid his debt to James I can be gauged by the fact that he was moved to the Tower and remained in prison for at least four and half years. In 1609 his wife Mary appealed to Salisbury successfully for the moiety of two of her husband's suspended crown annuities, but his final years were spent in great poverty. The government needed forgers, but it did not trust them.

Saints, sinners and prisoner priests

By contrast, Henry Garnet and Edward Oldcorne emerged from hiding to something approaching celebrity treatment. In Garnet's later account of his capture there is an element of relief, an end to furtiveness and an opportunity to face his persecutors. Salisbury noted that the new arrivals to the Gatehouse prison made no attempt to conceal their status 'themselves not sticking now to acknowledge their dignities'. Garnet later recalled his room in the Tower as 'a very fine chamber, but was very sick the first two nights with ill-lodging'.

In another nice piece of etiquette Lord Cobham, one of the chief suspects of the plots of 1603 who had been imprisoned in the Tower of London, also noted the new eminent arrivals to the Tower. He wrote to Salisbury to renew his suit for release, thinking perhaps that with Garnet's imprisonment the Gunpowder Plot crisis had subsided sufficiently to allow reconsideration of his case. Evidently he had not wished to trouble his brother-in-law with an old treason while he was preoccupied with a new one.

The comfort of Garnet's situation in the Tower was deceptive. The means of torture lay close at hand and his interrogators alternated high-flown theological debate with more direct cross-examination. Garnet began an elaborate game of cat and mouse with his captors. When initially examined he seemed entirely in control of the process, denying all knowledge of the plot before receiving Sir Everard Digby's letter seeking help on 6 November, and emphasizing that he had refused to help 'because they acted foolishly and wickedly'. He began to deny things which the authorities already knew from other sources.

IHS
Si quid patimini propter iustitiam, beati. 1. petri 3.
Henricus Garnetus anglus e societate IESV *passus*
3 May. 1606.

This suitably ambiguous image of Henry Garnet depicts a man both careworn and confident. Persecuted and under strain, he could still stay well ahead of his interrogators in argument (SP 14/216/218A).

While he replied cagily to his interrogators, Garnet found ingenious ways to communicate to his friends. He began to produce suspiciously small and inconsequential messages on suspiciously large sheets of paper. The legible part of an early letter from the Tower included a request for a pair of spectacles 'with a fold in the leather for your nose', presumably designed to alert the recipient to the fact that there was another way of looking at the letter. The real message was written on the back of the sheet in orange juice, which acted as an 'invisible ink', becoming visible when warmed. Garnet's letters were intercepted and deciphered, however, by one John Locherson, a government agent who befriended Garnet. Instead of smuggling the letters out, he passed them to the Lieutenant of the Tower, Sir William Waad. Once they had been deciphered by warming at the fire, they could not be passed on, so the originals survive in The National Archives and among Salisbury's papers at Hatfield House. Instead, copies were made and sent on in the hope of soliciting incriminating 'secret' replies from the recipients, which would also be intercepted. This first letter about spectacles contained Garnet's account of receiving Sir Everard Digby's letter at Coughton Court on 6 November, and described Mary Digby's tearful reaction to her husband's desperate plight. In a later 'orange juice' letter, Garnet commentated on the concealments and equivocations of his replies under interrogation and the weakness of the case against him: 'They have nothing against me but presumptions.' As time passed, his comments became less sanguine with the realization that in trials for treason presumptions were all the evidence required.

While it carefully warmed Garnet's orange juice letters and monitored his conversations, the government was always in danger of learning more than it wanted to know. In one of the many dubious overheard conversations in the Tower, in which Henry Garnet and Edward Oldcorne were left to talk together – apparently in private but with eavesdroppers stationed to listen – Northampton may have

THE INFORMERS' report on the conversations of Henry Garnet and Edward Oldcorne in the Tower, 25 February 1606. Garnet did not dispute the evidence obtained by this underhand method and believed the informers were 'honest fellows' (see transcription p.148).

matter. I said nothing of him, neither will I ever confess him. Then Garnett mentioned my Ld of Northumberland, my Ld of Rutland and one more (whom we heard not well) but to what effect they were named we could not hear by occasion of a Cock crowing under the window of the Room and the cackling of a Hen at the very same instant.

Saith Garnett, there is one special thing of which I doubted they would have taken an exact account of me; sc. of the cause's of my coming to Cawton which indeed would have bred a great suspicion of the matter. I will write to day or to-morrow [to whom we could not hear] to let them know that I am resolved to do my Lord no hurt.

Garnett used some words to this effect; [I hope they have yet no knowledge of the great &c.] But it was not well heard by either of us.

I will need take knowledge that you were with me at White Webbs. Then he told Hall of a Lease that was shewed him for taking of White Webbs and other words to that effect. You did not confess that we came together to Mrs Abington's for you know what we resolved upon. Then they seemed to think that they had failed in their several confessions for their meeting and about their Horses; and Garnett seemed to be very sorry that Hall held not better concurrence. But now they con=trived how to answer that point with more concurrence; sc. as if Garnett or Hall had misnamed one the other instead of a third person, whom they have now resolved upon. Garnett said "they went away been mentioned by Garnet in relation to the plot, but this and other uncomfortable facts were conveniently screened by a conspiracy of chickens. There is a lingering suspicion, however, that James's 'earwig', as the Earl of Northampton was sometimes unkindly known, could not be as loyal as he professed. Nobody could. The eavesdroppers heard the names of the earls of Northumberland and Rutland, with another whose name they could not hear.

25 FEBRUARY 1606: THE EAVESDROPPERS' REPORT

'Well I see they will justify my Lord Monteagle of all other matter. I said nothing of him, neither will I ever confess him.' There Garnet mentioned my Lord of Northumberland, my Lord of Rutland and one more (whom we heard not well), but to what effect they were named we could not hear by occasion of a cock crowing under the window of the room and the cackling of a hen at the very same instant. (SP 14/18/117)

Garnet had talked with an air of incredulity about the lengths to which the authorities were going to preserve the reputation of Lord Monteagle. Garnet implied that he could incriminate Monteagle but, given the attitude of the government, chose not to waste his breath. Breath spent implicating Northampton was likely to be equally wasted.

This is an almost comic reflection on the limitations of this particular form of sly government intelligence gathering. Would Northampton have been warned of the coming 'blow' in Parliament? If Catesby's attitude was anything to go by, he would not be esteemed by the conspirators. If the Lords in general were godless, Northampton was worse – a Catholic who attended Anglican services. However, his religion helped to make him an effective interrogator; he spoke Garnet's language and could use it against him. Northampton's learned approach, which tends to bore the general reader, nettled Garnet. His connections to prominent recusant families made him dangerous to them rather than to the king.

Northampton's speech at the trial of Sir Everard Digby had strained classical parallels to show the human betrayal as well as the political treason of which favoured men such as Digby had been guilty. The plot was presented as 'a Trojan horse, its belly stuffed

A portrait of Henry Howard, Earl of Northampton. 'His Majesty's Earwig' was a key figure in the investigation of the plot, and was also an important symbol of Catholic loyalty, but few of James's court really trusted him.

with hellish gunpowder'. Northampton wrote as loyally as he spoke. He composed much of the government's main case against the plotters, *A True and Perfect Relation*. But what were his private opinions, masked by the crowing of a cock?

While the government hid agents to eavesdrop on its prisoners,

The confession of Nicholas Oven taken the first of march 1605.

He confesseth that he hath at tymes attended and followed Henry Garnet the Provinciall of the Jesuits some fower yeares or thereaboute

He further saith that he this examinate was at the house of Thomas Throgmorton called Caughton in the beginning of November last when the lady Digby was there and by the watch that was in the Towne they did understand that Catesbie, Pearcy, and the rest of the Traytors were up in armes.

He also doth confesse that on Allhallowe day last Garnet did say masse at Caughton house at which masse this examinate was and some others to the number of half a dozen.

He further saith that the forenamed Henry Garnet als Wallie the Provinciall was at Henlipp the house of Thomas Abington some six weeke before the tyme that he was apprehended by Sr Henry Bromley, and Hall the Jesuite was there about three dayes before the house of Mr Abington was besett having bene there also before that tyme, and from thence the said Hall went into the Country for the space of a sevennight, and came againe as before is said some three dayes before the house was besett.

He also saith that during the foresaid tyme of six weeke he did attend on Mr Garnet to make his fyer, and to do those things which were fitt about him.

He saith further that the said Garnet did lye in a lower Chamber descending from the dyning Roome. And he also saith the said Garnet did ordinarylie dyne and suppe in the dyning chamber with Mr Abington and his wife and when Hall was there he did dyne and suppe there likewise.

He also doth confesse that he hath bene oftentymes with the said Garnet at the house called Whitewebbs in Enfield chare.

nicolas oven

Exam.

W. Waad

John Corbett

Robert Branthwaite

it gathered more evidence on the network of Jesuit priests in England. This gives us insight into the way in which laws against Catholic priests forced them, and the families who protected them, to live their lives in hiding and concealment. In many ways the figure who most closely embodies the plight of English Catholics and the besieged life of the landed Catholic families is Nicholas Owen, Jesuit lay brother, carpenter and servant to Henry Garnet, who made a career of devising hiding places and priest's holes in Catholic houses. Four days before Garnet's capture, Owen had been taken at Hindlip House, Worcestershire, in one of 'eleven secret corners and conveyances' which he himself had devised. Owen and his companion Ralph Ashley, a fellow lay brother, were starved out of a hide in the long gallery on 23 January 1606, after four days with one apple to eat between them. Owen's lower rank exposed him to harsher treatment from the authorities than his master received, but Garnet was nonetheless confident of his courage and loyalty: 'Little John', as Owen was known, would tell the authorities nothing. In Owen's initial examination he more than confirmed this hope, denying he knew Garnet at all.

Examined again on 1 March 1606, there is evidence that Owen, despite being lame after a kick from a horse and suffering from a hernia, was tortured; suspended by his thumbs while the questions were repeated to him, though his signature on this statement was neat and firm. The witnesses to his statement include no earls or others of rank overseeing his interrogation; as a lesser prisoner processed by the inferior commission, his interrogation could be harsher and more secret.

1 MARCH 1606: FINAL EXAMINATION OF NICHOLAS OWEN

The confession of Nicholas Owen taken the first of March 1605.

He confesseth that he hath at times attended and followed Henry Garnet the Provincial of the Jesuits some four years or thereabouts.

He further sayeth that he this examinate was at the house of Thomas

NICHOLAS OWEN's final examination, 1 March 1606. Owen's evidence gives interesting insight into priests' experiences in safe houses, including the terrifying raids and enforced cowering in cupboard-sized hiding places.

Throgmorton called Coughton at the beginning of November last when the Lady Digby was there and by the watch that was in the town they did understand that Catesby, Percy and the rest of the Traitors were up in arms.

(SP 14/216/194)

This time Owen admitted serving Garnet and being at Coughton Court when the Midlands rebellion took place. Even here, however, he gave less information than Garnet had already supplied, not mentioning Sir Everard Digby's letter calling for aid, but rather insisting that he had heard of the rebellion by 'general report' via the 'watch' (a local law officer).

Unsurprisingly, his interrogators were not impressed with his answers and he was threatened that he would be racked on the next occasion. Owen contrived to free himself of his keeper by complaining of the coldness of his broth. When the keeper had gone to warm it, he apparently stabbed himself with a knife which had been deliberately blunted as a precaution against suicide. Other reports after his death asserted that he had died on the rack. We may think that whether his death was by torture or the threat of it makes little moral difference. It was, in a way, a victory, however; he had told the authorities nothing they did not already know. Though Owen's low rank contributed to the manner of his death, his courage and conviction were to earn him sainthood centuries later. He was beatified by Pope Pius XI on 15 December 1929 and canonized by Paul VI on 25 October 1970.

The Earl of Northumberland was imprisoned on rather easier terms, and on the day after Owen's death might even have been in hope of an impending release. Salisbury wrote to Monteagle's brother-in-law Lord Brounker, expressing hope that Northumberland would 'come to liberty on easy terms' because the government lacked men of 'blood and sufficiency'. There is an indication here that figures of noble birth and ability were a rare commodity, and the pragmatic realization that the government could not insist on absolute loyalty and still hope to find sufficient numbers of the calibre and social standing required. The earl certainly received better treatment than many of the prisoners – his keepers, Sir William and Lady Waad, sent Northumberland cheeses in the Tower.

There seemed to be some tension in the government as to what should best be done with the suspected lords. Coke wanted the nobles to face the full severity of trial at common law as the principal plotters had done, while James, following the pattern of his Scottish reign, wanted them fined and grateful under the more discretionary and personal powers of the Court of Star Chamber. Despite their periodic rebelliousness, James relied on Catholic noblemen in England as he had in Scotland, and generally found them more politically and socially acceptable than those who shared his religious views.

In a long letter dated 'Shrove Tuesday' (4 March 1606), Henry Garnet gave Anne Vaux a full and witty account of his arrest and interrogation. Annotated 'keep all discreetly secret', it gave details of life in a priest's hole, immobile for seven days and nights. Garnet implied that he and Edward Oldcorne had been forced to give themselves up only by the conditions in their hiding place. They could have held out much longer if they had had a toilet; 'having a close stool, we could have hidden a quarter of a year'. The searchers when they discovered them were more frightened than the priests, thinking the deadly Jesuits would be armed with pistols. The result – an ironic reflection on the standard of local law enforcement – was a vast crowd of gawping men assembled to secure two middle-aged clergymen who could barely walk.

4 March 1606: In the priest's hole – letter from Henry Garnet to Anne Vaux

The fellow that found us ran away for fear, thinking we would have shot a pistol at him, but there came needless company to assist him and we bad them 'be quiet and we would come forth'. So they helped us out very charitably.

(SP 14/19/11)

Despite the seriousness of the situation, Garnet writes of the comedy of his own position and the nature of the pursuing forces – which, as at Holbeach, do not sound like the inexorable arm of a police state. Garnet and Oldcorne were carried to Worcester as prisoners, just as the survivors of Holbeach had been. Sir Henry Bromley, who had led the search for Garnet as an enemy of the

...s Anne. ...of ours ...keep all ...ly secret.

Jhesus Maria

Shrovetues[day]

I purpose by Gods grace, to sett downe here briefly, what hath passed since my apprehensio, least euill reports or vntruths, may do my self or others iniury.

After we had bene in the houle, 7. dayes, & 7. nights, & some odd howres: every man may well think we were well wearyed. & in deed so it was; for we cotinually satte, save that some times we could half stretch or selves, the place being not high enough. & we had or legges so straightened, that we could not sitting, find place for them, so that we both were in cotinuall paine of or legges: & both or legges especially mine, were much swollen, & mine cotinued so till I came to the tower. If we had had but one half day liberty to come forth, we had so eased ye place fro bookes, & furniture, that having with vs a close stole, we could have abidden a quarter of a yeare. For that all my ffrends will wonder at, especially in me that neither of vs went to the stole, all the while, though we had meanes to do servitij piccoli: whereof also we were at a nonplus, the day of or taking.

We were very merry & cotent within: & hard the searchers every day most curious over vs, wch made me in deed think ye place would be found. And if I had knowne in time of ye proclamation against me, I would have come forth, & offred my self to [illegible] whether he would or no, to have bene his prisoner.

When we came forth, we appeared like 2. ghosts, yet I the strongest, though my weakenes lasted longest. The fellow that found vs ranne away for feare, thinking we would have shotte a pistoll at him. but there came needlesse copany to assist him. & we bad them be quiett, & we would come forth. so they holpe vs out very charitably. & we could not go but desyred to be lead to a house of office. So I was: & found a bord taken vp, where there was a great downfall, that one should have broaken his neck, if he had come thither in the dark. wch seemed intended of purpose. We had escaped, if ye 2. first [illegible] souldiers, had not come out so soone: for when they found them, they were curious to find their place.

state at Hindlip, immediately took him to dinner. Later popular calumny harped on Garnet's love of wine as if he were a drunkard, which he was not, but he does devote almost an entire page of a four-page letter (justifying his actions to the faithful through Anne Vaux) to describing the wines on offer at Sir Henry's table. Ben Jonson's *Volpone* re-told the gossip about Garnet with a characteristically ambiguous twist: 'I have heard / The rack hath cured the gout,' observes the advocate Voltore in the course of suggesting how to treat the captured miscreant Volpone, implying that Garnet had indeed been tortured, but that it had done him good by curing the symptoms of his drunkenness. Neither Garnet's apologists nor his enemies would admit both parts of this rumour; perhaps Jonson wished to present them both as equally untrustworthy.

The government set about confronting Garnet and Oldcorne in turn with elements of each others' testimony which contradicted what they themselves had said, in the hope of extracting fuller confessions. They succeeded to some extent, but also threatened to confuse themselves. Both testimonies agreed on the one unacceptable fact that Lord Monteagle had been heavily involved in negotiations for a Spanish invasion before 1603. Oldcorne co-operatively downgraded this from fact to opinion in his evidence by the insertion of 'as I think' in his hand. However, he later confirmed he had done this only because the nature of his questioning made it clear this was what his questioners wanted.

On 8 March 1606 came Garnet's evidence, endorsed by Salisbury 'forbidden by the K[ing] to be given in evidence'. It stated that Monteagle believed decisive action might still need to be taken against King James as late as the summer of 1605. At a meeting with Monteagle and Tresham at a house in Essex in the summer of 1605, all parties agreed that James was 'odious'.

Oldcorne subsequently shed further light on the gunpowder explosion at Holbeach. He had reassured the plotters that in his

HENRY GARNET's letter to Anne Vaux, 4 March 1606. This witty and self-deprecating account paints a picture of a likeable, middle-aged theologian – as uneasy with those who wanted to make him a martyr as with those seeking his execution (see transcription p.153).

considered theological opinion the gunpowder explosion and the failure of the plot could not, after all, be interpreted as signs of divine displeasure:

> After Mr Catesby saw himself and others in the company burnt with powder, and the rest of the company ready to fly from him, that then he began to think he had offended God in this action, seeing so bad effects follow from the same. I answered him that an act is not to be condemned or justified upon the good or bad events that followeth it. The Christians defended Rhodes against the Turks and the Christians were overthrown.

This was just the kind of evidence that the government sought. They were keen to show that the plotters, superstitious but beaten men who might otherwise have been recalled to their obedience by misfortune, had had their resolve stiffened by the sinister, hidden hand of foreign-trained priests. In the end, however, the distinction the government tried to make between the potentially loyal English Catholics and their treasonous priests was not sustainable, for it was impossible to practise religion without priests. The life of criminality which fidelity to Catholicism involved is well illustrated by Henry Garnet's correspondent in orange juice, Anne Vaux. Well connected and wealthy, she was the daughter of William, third Baron Vaux of Harrowden. She was eight years old when the bull of Pope Pious freed English Catholics from their allegiance to a heretic monarch (at that time, Elizabeth I). It divided English Catholics from their compatriots, ushering in legislation which implied, as Sir Everard Digby had complained in his letter to Salisbury, 'that only to be a Catholic is to be a traitor'. Anne lived her life at the centre of a recusant household, showing considerable courage and resolve in protecting priests, especially Henry Garnet.

'Many Great Protestations'

The description of Anne by Sir Thomas Tresham, father of Francis, as a 'virtuous and zealous Catholic maiden' comes from his appraisal of her character as 'reported' by other people, based on her 'exterior show'. It is, in fact, part of a prolonged denunciation of her conduct, both in extorting money from him when he is in prison and in slandering him. It is pretty clear that the two, though related (Tresham's sister Mary was Anne's stepmother) and Catholic, disliked one another intensely. We have sometimes a romantic idea that persecution had turned this network of Catholic families into a homogeneous mass of loyalty and devotion, but in reality they were as divided, jealous and competitive as anyone else. Ties of blood were considered strong circumstantial evidence by the authorities, but sometimes they concealed only mutual distrust. The documents connected to Anne Vaux's role in the plot also show very human motivation in the language of piety.

Anne and her widowed sister Eleanor showed considerable resource and courage in sheltering missionary priests in various safe houses. These included White Webbs, the house 'this side of Theobalds' which Fawkes had named as a base for the conspirators. During the summer of 1605 Anne accompanied Garnet and others, including Ambrose Rookwood and his family, on a pilgrimage to St Winifred's Well (Holywell) in Flintshire. Garnet himself confirmed that despite the plotters' attempts to remain 'monastical' and exclude women from the secret of the plot, Anne was quite bright and observant enough to realize something was up. Several Gunpowder Plot conspirators visited White Webbs that summer and autumn, and on the way to Holywell she had noted the 'fine horses' in the Wintours' and Grant's stables. She later recalled how she had 'feared these wild heads had something in hand', and asked Garnet to dissuade Catesby from any rash attempt. On first being examined by the authorities Anne remained conspicuously loyal to Garnet, denying he was on the pilgrimage to Holywell even though he led it.

She concealed the fugitive Garnet after the proclamation for his arrest and followed him to London when he was arrested. There she responded in kind to Garnet's letters in invisible ink. Her letters, like Garnet's to her, were intercepted. While in secret correspondence with Garnet she protested in a very different tone to the authorities of Garnet's deception:

> I am most sorry to hear that Father Garnet should be one year privy to this most wicked action as he himself ever called it, for that he made me many great protestations to the contrary divers times since.

BADDESLEY CLINTON (above), one of the houses rented by Anne Vaux. The moat gave valuable extra seconds for priests to hide from their pursuers. An 'orange juice' letter (right) from Anne Vaux to Garnet after his capture, 21 March 1606. She replied in kind to his coded messages, but their intimacy was broken by the interception of the letters.

There is no loss of trust or lack of intimacy in their 'secret' correspondence, even after Anne was arrested in March. Before, during and after the period of Anne's questioning by the authorities the 'secret' correspondence continued. An 'orange juice' letter to Garnet, tentatively dated 21 March 1606, showed that she wrote better than he does using it, in recognizably her handwriting, while he appears to be squeezing directly on to the paper. She seems to have complete confidence in him while she can communicate securely, and betrays none of the doubt in him she expresses to the authorities.

21 MARCH 1606: LETTER FROM ANNE VAUX TO HENRY GARNET IN ORANGE JUICE

My hope is that you will continue your care of me and commend me to some that will for your sake help me for life without you is not life but death, now I see my loss I am and ever will be yours and so humbly beseech you to account me. O that I might see you! (SP 14/216/244)

5

on Saturday at supper the aturne sead
that when you yeare in excamening you
fened your selfe sike to goo to your cam
ber and coming and coming thether you
seme to ~~att~~ take sumo marmelate which
euen then was sent you and burned a
letter which your keeper seing did tel ~~an~~
and you being excamened sead that it
yas a leter ~~that~~ a frend had sent you
and fering that ther meight be anethi
ng of danger to the partey you burned
it and that you had aknoleged that
you know of the powther action but
not a pratteser in it. the paper sent you
with the Box was concerning my self
if this cum safe to you I will wryte and so
will more frendes who wolde be
glad to haue derection from you
who should supply your roume for myselfe
I am forced to seeke new frendes my
olde are wosearels of nee I beseche you
for god sake advies me what cours to
take so long as I ma here from you
not out of Lundon my hope i that you will
contenew your care of me and commen
dme to sum that will for your sake help
mee I whene with out you it is not life but
deathe now I see my los I am and euer
willbe yours and so I humbly beseche
you to acounte me so that I meight
see you
yours

208

A REPORT of the trial of Henry Garnet in special oyer and terminer roll and file. With less firm evidence than against the core plotters, Garnet's trial became still more theatrical (KB 8/61).

Whatever the nature of their love, there seems little doubt that that is what it was. The authorities occasionally suggested their love was physical, only to retract in embarrassment and apology. Popular calumny, always keen on such stories, took up the suggestion eagerly.

Drowning Sorrow

Quite suddenly, on 22 March 1606, there came a rumour that James had been slain hunting at Woking, widely enough credited to require a proclamation to refute. John Chamberlain wrote to Dudley Carleton with details of the proclamation on 27 March, and on the same day Carleton wrote to him from Oxfordshire that the report of the king's death had been generally believed. Both obviously wrote as soon as it was safely confirmed that the king was unharmed.

Along with the story of the king's survival came another nugget of news which Chamberlain was able to send his friend from the capital: that of Henry Garnet's forthcoming trial.

> Garnet is to be arraigned this day at Guildhall with great concourse. I doubt he will deceive their expectation, for I am of opinion he will say little: once he hath been very indulgent to himself both in the gatehouse and in the Tower, and daily drunk sack so liberally as if he meant to drown sorrow.

Sir William Waad was also concerned about the physical condition of his prisoner and the practical arrangements for getting him to Guildhall: 'the way is longer from the Tower and Garnet is no good footman'. Waad was also concerned that his own place at the trial should be in keeping with his rank and the importance of the services he had rendered the state. The trials following the discovery of the plot were great theatrical social occasions which drew large paying crowds, sometimes too many to allow important people the prominent places they wanted. It is also evident from the reporting of the trials that they were theatrical in another sense, being show rather than substance. No one appears to have expected new compelling evidence, or revelations which might upset the course of the trial, it was simply a chance to see the notorious defendants at first hand and comment on their behaviour before the inevitable verdict and sentence.

In the days before Henry Garnet's trial the government was busy gathering evidence against him, but much of what they took from Anne Vaux was not what they were looking for. Passages in her evidence were underlined as not to be used in the trial because they showed Garnet's attempts to keep the plotters 'quiet'. While the government was keen to suppress such straightforward – and probably accurate – evidence which did not accord with their theories, they were also coming to doubt the veracity of any evidence taken from witnesses familiar with the doctrine of equivocation which Garnet had expounded. Three months after his death, it appeared that Francis Tresham had retracted on his deathbed his implication of Garnet in past plots. Sir Edward Coke, who was constructing evidence for Garnet's trial designed to show that he had been behind every Catholic plot since 1588, noted that Tresham's retraction was full of 'manifest falsehoods'. Nevertheless, the retraction made the authorities uneasy about the reliance which might be placed on such witnesses.

Garnet contributed to government unease by continuing to implicate Lord Monteagle in attempts by the papacy to secure a Catholic succession in England in 1603. Garnet protested he burnt papal directions about the succession and the inadmissibility of a Protestant monarch on James's succession, but had shown them to Robert Catesby first. He added that Catesby had shown them to Monteagle. On the following day, however, Garnet 'did not remember' that Monteagle had seen them – an obvious indication of the pressure applied to Garnet to forget a Monteagle connection.

While William Waad and the audience haggled about their places at Garnet's trial, Salisbury sent a note to Sir Edward Coke reminding him of his lines.

28 March 1606: Salisbury's instructions to Sir Edward Coke on the conduct of Garnet's trial

First that you be sure to make it appear, to the world, that there was an employment of some person to Spain for a practice of invasion as soon as the queen's breath was out of her body.

... you must deliver in commendation of my Lord Monteagle, words to show how sincerely he dealt and how fortunate it proved that he was the agent of so great a blessing as this was. (SP 14/19/94)

On the whole, Salisbury's instructions smack of a desire to keep Coke on message rather than a sinister attempt to pervert the evidence. He gives reasons for all his instructions, chiefly to counteract rumour of Monteagle's direct involvement in the Gunpowder Plot – 'it is lewdly given out that he is one of this plot of powder' – and to deny that one of the convicted plotters wrote the Monteagle letter, to prevent any of them confusing the issue by sharing in

A portrait of Sir Edward Coke by Flemish artist Marcus Gheeraerts. As Attorney General at the time of the plot, Coke was zealous in pursuing figures beyond the core plotters. Sometimes his agenda seemed to run beyond the control of Salisbury and the king.

ward Coke
Chief Justice

These things I am comanded to recom vnto yor memory/

First yt you be sure to make it appeare, to ye world, yt there was an Imployment of some psons to spaine, for a practise of Invasion, assoon as ye q. breath was out of her body/

The reason is this, for wch ye k. doth urge it. he sayth some men there are yt will give owt, and do, yt only dispaire of ye k's courses in ye catholicks, and his severity drave all these to such woorks of discontentment, whereby you It will appeare, yt before his Mtie Face was seen or yt he had don any Thing in governmt the k. of sp: was moved, thogh he refused it, saying he rather expected to have peace. et cet.

Next you must in any case, when you speake of ye lre wch was ye first grownd of discovery, absolutly disclame yt any of these wrote it, though you leave ye further Iudgment indefinite who els it should be/

Lastly and yt you must not omitt, you must deliver in comendation of my L. Mownt

Monteagle's glory 'though you leave the further subject indefinite, who else it should be'. Yet who else could it be? The government preferred to present the letter as divine agency.

Coke continued to ignore large parts of these instructions. Salisbury, seen by many as the great manipulator of the plot, could not even rely on the Attorney General to present the government view consistently. Coke was very keen on pursuing suspect lords, men who might think themselves above the law, and would have been quite eager to have prosecuted Monteagle. He was not about to praise him. The lack of an established pattern to the plot gave the commissioners scope to adopt their own private theories, perhaps another reason why Salisbury finds a consistent government line difficult to sustain and why it seems to shift suspiciously.

Garnet's trial in the Guildhall began on 28 March. Coke pursued his own agenda and his own rhetorical manner of proceeding, using poetic linguistic devices to lend weight to arguments which were by no means conclusive of guilt. Coke presented Garnet as the instigator of the plot and showed he must be devilishly inspired because he was guilty of so many things beginning with 'd'. Garnet, said Coke,

> hath many gifts and endowments of nature, by art learned, a good linguist and, by profession, a Jesuit and a Superior as indeed he is Superior to all his predecessors in devilish treason, a Doctor of Dissimulation, Deposing of Princes, Disposing of Kingdoms, Daunting and deterring of subjects, and Destruction.

Garnet defended himself against all Coke's charges and explained Catholic teaching on papal power and equivocation, on which Coke had attempted to place a sinister construction during the trial. Yet a treason trial was always ultimately a tragedy rather than a comedy – the charges so grave that a reprieve was almost impossible. The court found Garnet guilty as charged and sentenced him to death.

After his conviction Garnet continued to write to his various correspondents, but without some of the assurance and social ease that had marked his early interrogations. This was not simply the

This remarkable document, dated 28 March 1606, contains Salisbury's explicit instructions to Sir Edward Coke about how to conduct Garnet's trial. More remarkable still was how Coke ignored them (transcription p.162).

result of the seriousness of his predicament. His captors lied to him about the scandal his conduct had caused among Catholics, in admitting his knowledge of the plot and implicating Oswald Tesimond in his absence. They lied, too, about the 'capture' of Oswald Tesimond and his supposed testimony, which was said to undermine Garnet's. In fact Tesimond was still free and would live to put his name to a narrative justifying Garnet. The government's tactics were underhand but successful; Garnet became defensive and uneasy in his communications about the plot with his fellow Catholics. He wrote to Anne Vaux of his mystical vision of their place in heaven, but quickly followed it with justifications of his conduct; their implicit trust is somewhat undermined. He then wrote a rather uneasy note to the supposedly captive Tesimond, explaining his conduct in casting some of the blame on him while he believed him to be free. Sir William Waad believed there was sufficient discrepancy between Garnet's various statements 'to disclose his hypocrisy' in order to disillusion Anne Vaux. Sir Thomas Edmondes reported from Brussels that Garnet's obvious contradictions were evident even to his supporters in the city; there, however, they were explained away as proof that he had been tortured.

In fact, the unease with which Garnet dealt with his Catholic allies contrasted with his relationship with his interrogators – in general rather cordial. In 'a declaration for the King to see', Garnet acknowledged his fault in not revealing what he knew of Catesby's 'general intention' outside the seal of confession, which showed that he was still in hope of earning a reprieve although under sentence of death. Among the Cecil papers at Hatfield House is a note from Garnet deploring Catesby's deception in taking his name in vain to persuade others his scheme had been sanctioned – with the consequence that Garnet's role in the plot seemed more central than it was. By contrast, he treats his evidence to the commissioners and their attempts to trick him as something of a game. He knew, he says, both that the 'orange juice' letters were intercepted and his

GARNET's final letter to Anne Vaux, dated 21 April 1606, shows him as an unlikely spymaster. Able to outwit his captors in theological argument, he was lured by misinformation into revealing details of his network of safe houses.

I thought verely my chambs in James Street had bene geven over: & therefore I used it to save Erith: but I might have done otherwise.

It pleaseth God dayly to multiply my Crosses. I beseech him geve me patience & perseverance usq in finem.

I was aft[er] a weeks hyding taken in a ffrends house, where o[ur] Confessions & secret conferences were heard & my letters taken, by some indiscreetd abroade. then the taking of yo[ur]self. after, my arraignment: then the taking of M[r] Greenwell: then the slaunder of us both abroade: then the ransacking a new of Erith & the other house. ~~& now~~ then the executio[n] of M[r] Hall: & now last of all the apprehensio[n] of Richard & Robert with a cifer I know not of whose layed to my charge: & that w[hi]ch was a singuler oversight, a lett[er] written in cifer together with the cifer: w[hi]ch letter may bring many into questio[n]. Sufferentiam Iob audistis et finem Domini vidistis, quoniam misericors Dominus est et miserator.

Sit nomen Domini Benedictum. 21 Apr

Yours in æternum as I hope. H. G.

IHS

Deus cordis mei: et pars mea Deus in æternum.

conversations with Oldcorne overheard, but even the eavesdroppers he reports as 'honest fellows, though they could not hear us clearly'. Nor is Garnet's relationship with Salisbury, as he records it, exactly what you would expect between the principal secretary and public enemy number one:

> I never had a discourteous word of the commissioners but only once, when they having taken a letter of Mrs Vaux to me subscribed 'your loving sister A.G.' my Lord Salisbury said 'What, are you married to Mrs Vaux, she calls herself Garnet? What! Senex fornicarius [You dirty old man].' But the next time he asked me forgiveness and said he spoke in jest, and held his arm long on my shoulders; and all the rest said that I was held for exemplar in those matters.

Both sides seem to have been more worried by the impropriety of the remark than actually discovering why Anne Vaux should sign a letter 'A.G.' Garnet's self-deprecation and disavowal of martyrdom made him an unlikely figure for veneration, but also a difficult man for his oppressors to hate. It was also clear that the role of conspiracist did not suit him. His final letter to Anne Vaux is that of a man overtaken by events and bemoaning his own ineptitude in guile and secrecy:

21 April 1606: Garnet's last letter to Anne Vaux

It pleaseth God to multiply my crosses. I beseech him give me patience and perseverance usque in finem. I was after a week's hiding taken in a friend's house, where our confessions and secret conferences were heard, and my letters taken by some indiscretion abroad; then the taking of yourself; after my arraignment; then the taking of Mr Greenwell [*another alias of Tesimond*]; *then the slander of us both abroad; then the ransacking anew of Erith and the other house; then the execution of Mr Hall and now last of all the apprehension of Richard and Robert; with a cipher, I know not of whose laid to my charge, and that which was a singular oversight, a letter written in cipher, together with the cipher; which letter may bring many into question.*

Suffer etiam hos; audistis et finem Domini vidistis; quemadmodum misericors Dominus est et miserator. Sit nomen Domini benedictum.
Yours in aeternum as I hope H G'

I thought verily my chamber in Thames Street had been given over therefore I used it to save Erith; but I might have done otherwise. (SP 14/20/39)

Garnet does not exactly present an image of wronged innocence. The impression is rather of a scholarly theologian, forced by his position and anti-Catholic legislation to assume a spymaster's role. Why did he not tell what he knew from sources other than the confessional of Catesby's 'general intention'? The government view was that this was because he was the secret power behind the plot, urging the plotters on, but this is scarcely borne out by his other actions. Like everybody else, Garnet evidently liked Catesby and, as Francis Tresham had done, believed that there might be other ways than outright betrayal to prevent the plot. His position was that of many persecuted groups in society before and since, for whom going to the authorities was a last resort.

Garnet's execution was first deferred to avoid the overtones of martyrdom conferred by Easter, or 'holy week as they call it', as Salisbury put it. It was then delayed again to avoid the possibility of disorder if it were held on May Day. Dudley Carleton wrote to John Chamberlain on 2 May, expressing little fellow feeling for another suspect.

2 May 1606: Hanging without equivocation

Garnet should have come a-maying to the gallows which was set up for him in Paul's Church Yard on Wednesday but upon better advice his execution is put off until tomorrow for fear of disorder amongst prentices and others in a day of such misrule. The news of his death was sent him upon Monday last by Dr Abbott, which he could hardly be persuaded to believe, having conceived great hope of grace by some good words and promises he said were made to him and by the Spanish Ambassador's mediation who he thought would have spoken to the King for him. He hath since often been visited and examined by the Attorney, who finds him shifting and faltering in all his answers; and it is looked he will equivocate at the gallows; but he will be hanged without equivocation, though yet some think he should have favour upon a petitionary letter he hath sent to the King. (SP14/21/4)

There are various social currents flowing here which might strike a modern reader as odd. First, the fact that the hanging of a middle-aged clergyman was in danger of becoming a popular festival or even a scene of popular unrest, and second that Garnet could, as a

Sr I returned no answeare by yr messinger that came from Ware parke because I imagined you would then be gone to Knebworth. Ever since I have bin a housekeeping and scarce stird out of dores, so as I can send you little newes, unless you will be content with such as my sister williams hath gathered together in her visits. and first you may understand that mres Doctor of Aldermary church is brought to bed of a goodly daughter, wch her husband tooke almost as a miracle: for in open audience of his gossips he made it a great wonder it should be so great since he had taken so small paynes for it. Sr Tho: Stukely came to towne about a weeke since, and upon a Tabacco sicknes sent up for his wife in post. who brought up her great belly behind one of her men in a day and a half. upon sight of her he recovered. and here they are for a fortnight at least, not a little busied in borrowing and broking for mony to pay for a purchase they have made of a manor of my Ld: Lisles in hampshire, wch cost them 4000li. It was lookt yesterday that Garnet should have come a maying to the gallows wch was set up for him in Paules church yard on wednesday. but upon better advise it his execution is putt of till tomorrow, for feare of disorder amongest prentises and others in a day of such misrule: The newes of his death was sent him upon monday last by D: Abbots, wch he would hardly be perswaded to believe, having conceived great hope of grace by some goode words and promises he sayde were made him: and by the Spanish Ambassadors mediation who he thought would have spoken to ye K: for him. He hath bin since often visited and examined by the Atturny, who finds him shifting and faltering in all his answeares, and it is lookt he will equivocate at ye gallows, but he will be ~~[illegible]~~ hangd wthout equivocation fugitive and then a condemned man, apparently remain on such good terms with the most important ambassador at James's court. He appears also to have had an amicable relationship outside the courtroom with Sir Edward Coke, the man prosecuting him. Coke scarcely needed last minute evidence from Garnet for the hatchet job he was preparing, and had no reason other than interest or a reluctant admiration to pay so many calls on the priest. Garnet even had grounds to expect mercy from the king. While official polemic singled out the Jesuits as the intellectual force behind the plot, the reaction to Garnet as an individual priest was rather more ambiguous. His interrogators refused to recognize his priesthood, calling him 'Mister Garnet' in their examinations, but they still asked him to swear 'on his priesthood' in the hope of procuring truthful evidence, and doffed their hats in cross-examining him.

Garnet's fate, however, was sealed. Like the conspirators he was hung, drawn and quartered, on 3 May 1606 in St Paul's churchyard, and his remains were dispersed to avoid creating a shrine. English Catholics began to venerate Garnet as a martyr, despite his own assertion that he was no martyr but 'a penitent thief'. Among the many relics associated with him was a husk of straw taken from the place of execution, on which was a drop of Garnet's blood which bore a strong resemblance to his face. The straw

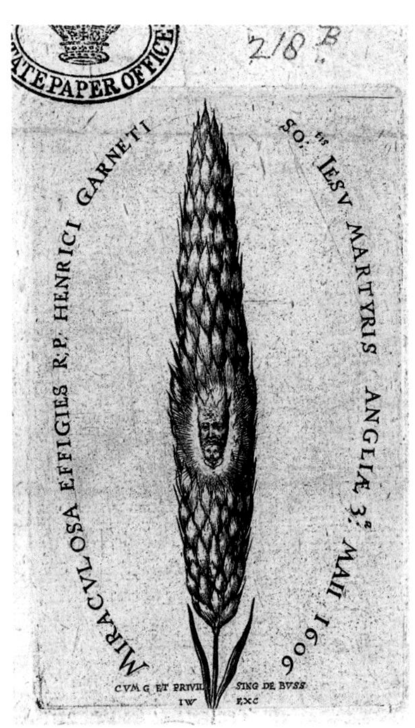

DUDLEY CARLETON's letter to John Chamberlain (left), 2 May 1606, was jocular about Garnet's coming execution (see transcription p. 169). A representation of Garnet's straw (above), which carried a drop of his blood miraculously supposed to be in his image (SP 14/216/218B).

was eventually smuggled out of the kingdom and kept at the English Jesuit college in Liège, but was lost during the French Revolution. Anne Vaux was released from prison in August 1606, and was in part responsible for publicizing 'Garnet's straw'. One of Salisbury's contacts, Thomas Wilson, wrote in alarm that White Webbs was to be leased to Anne Vaux again after Garnet's execution and the sale of his possessions. 'This I tell you because it is next neighbour to Theobalds, and unfit it should be again a nest for such bad birds as it was before.'

The End of the 'Plot of Powder'

Among the many commentators who agreed that no new evidence had come out of Garnet's trial was Sir Allan Percy, brother of the Earl of Northumberland and his lieutenant of the gentlemen pensioners. Sir Allan had attempted to help his brother by insisting that he, as lieutenant, had administered the oath of loyalty to Thomas Percy, only for it to be proved that he could not have done so when he said. In a letter dated 1 April, Allan Percy commented on Garnet's trial to Dudley Carleton. He noted that the earl's position seemed to have worsened while attention had been fixed on Garnet. The earl had not been mentioned by the commissioners at the trial 'yet there was a show as though they could say more than they would'. The earl was in their thoughts, and the case against him was growing.

After months of rumour but with no firm evidence beyond the circumstantial, Northumberland was charged, and in June 1606 tried in the Court of Star Chamber. This effectively thwarted Coke's desire to try the suspect lords by common law as the principal plotters had been, giving the king greater scope to dispense personal justice according to social rank. Northumberland was found guilty of three offences for which he was fined £10,000 each: pretending to lead the Catholic party in England (an offence against rank, assuming royal power in leading men not bound to him in service); employing Percy in the bodyguard; and failing to order Thomas Percy's apprehension as the plot's prime suspect when sending to the North about his rents on 5 November. He was condemned to imprisonment during the king's pleasure and in fact remained in the

Tower until June 1621. As a man of 'blood and sufficiency', there was always hope of reprieve in this period, but none came. He was potentially too important a figure to be released. The earl began to entertain notions of conspiracy against him centred on the political jealousy of the Earl of Salisbury, but Salisbury's death was to make no difference. The prisoner occupied his time quietly and profitably in reading and experiment, those private recreations that he had claimed were his only ambition. On his release, he withdrew from the affairs of state. Northumberland attracted little sympathy in any quarter; his behaviour was too suspicious and his manner too abrasive. Some commentators did, however, suggest that he had suffered more than he might have done because of the rebellious reputation of the 'Gunpowder Percys'.

After his own trial in the Star Chamber on 3 June 1606, Edward, Lord Stourton – one of the lords suspected of having been warned not to attend Parliament by Catesby – was committed to the Tower. From here he wrote a plea for liberty to Salisbury: 'I crave my speedy enlargement, in pity of my health and my decaying estate, unable to support so great charges and supply the wants of so many children.' This prompted only a transfer to quarters in the Fleet prison, serving to indicate that his offence was being regarded less seriously without necessarily improving the prospects for his health. Moved with him was Henry, Lord Mordaunt. Both were released in 1608, and the fines against them were not enforced. Mordaunt died in 1609 and used his will, written despite 'languishing sickness (the messenger of death)' after long imprisonment, to protest his innocence of the plot with a dramatic, dying breath:

> And for the clearing of my conscience before God and man and to give a public satisfaction to the world concerning such and those imputations which lately have been laid upon me, and for which I have in an high degree been censured, I mean the late Gunpowder Treason, which fact for the heinousness thereof in the offenders therein, I do loathe to remember and now sorrow to repeat: Therefore at this time when all hope or desire of long life hath forsaken me and now Almighty God (into whose hands I am instantly yielding my soul) is my immediate judge to witness with me that I lie not, I do solemnly protest before God and his Angels and without all Equivocation or duplicity whatsoever that I am innocent of that fact and guiltless of all foreknowledge thereof.

The government had heard protestations of this sort before. As Mordaunt and Stourton were moved to the Fleet, Anthony Maria Browne, Lord Montagu, was released. In 1611 he made a £6,000 payment of lieu of recusancy fines and not to be tendered the oath of allegiance. If you were rich enough, it seemed, you need not face the inconvenience of choosing between your loyalty to king or pope.

'Sooner dead than changed': the legacy of John Donne

Most people were not in this position, however. The complexity of Catholic loyalty, and the difficulty of the choices they were compelled to make, is illustrated by the poet John Donne, an exact contemporary of Robert Catesby, whose Catholic childhood had been filled with the same scare stories of murderous decrees from the Privy Council. Donne's family and connections were Catholic and long-suffering; he had Jesuit uncles and he had visited William Weston, Garnet's predecessor as Superior of the English Jesuit Province, in the Tower at the age of 12. His brother Henry was arrested for harbouring a priest in Lincoln's Inn and died of plague in Newgate before he could come to trial. For the young Donne, a short life ending in martyrdom beckoned; perhaps he was even a plotter in the making. As a young man he travelled in Catholic countries including Spain and, like Thomas Wintour, he picked up cultural influences closed to most of his fellow Englishmen. He appears in an engraving by William Marshall dated 1591 as a fashionable young man tinged with the experience and sophistication of his travels, wearing ear-rings in the shape of crosses and holding an ornate sword. The portrait carries the Spanish motto *antes muerto que mudado* – 'sooner dead than changed'. Here, it seemed, was a man like 'Guido' Fawkes, ready to die rather than adopt the orthodoxies of the English. His early poems seem to bear out some of

A DOCUMENT from the legal dispute between Sir Thomas Overbury and John Talbot as the family tried to secure Wintour's 'attainted' property after his death. Wintour in his last days imagined his descendants avenging him in unending religious struggle, but they sought rather to save the remains of his estates by legal means (E 134/7JAS1/EAST30).

... Saunders and so did the said m[r] Barrotts ... at perill followinge) which was the moneth of November in the said third yeare of his ma[jes]ties Raigne before which day appointed the said Robte Wintour brake forth into open Rebellion and by reason thereof the said deeds were not sealed nor delivered and all this this depon[en]t knoweth to be true because he ingrossed the said books and was not paid for the same.

ex p[ar]te def[endentis] Leonard Smallpeece of [illegible] in the Com[itatu] of Salop gent of the age of fiftie foure yeares or thereabouts sworne and examined saith as hereafter followeth.

1 To the first inter[rogatory] he saith that he doth not know the compl[ainant]. But he doth well know the said John Talbott Gertrude Wintour Edward Barrott the elder Edward Barrott the younger and Robte Barrott.

2 To the second inter[rogatory] he deposeth and saith that he did know Robte Wintour Thomas Wintour John Wintour and John Talbott of Longford and John Grant in that inter[rogatory] mentioned and he doth know John Talbott of Grafton esquire and Edward Cookes likewise in that inter[rogatory] mentioned.

3 To the third inter[rogatory] he deposeth and saith That he doth know that the said Robte Wintour about the two and fortieth yeare of the Raigne of our late Queene Elizabeth was seised in his demesne as of fee of one in five and twenty Bullaries of salt water with the appurtenances in Droitwich in the County of Worcester and that the same as this depon[en]t verilie thinketh were all in upper wiche in Droitwich in the County aforesaid And that he was seised of foure and twenty of the said Bullaries from Trinity terme in the said xlij[o] yeare of the Raigne of our said Soveraigne Ladie Queene Elizabeth.

4 To the fourth he saith that the said Robte Wintour was seised of xxiiij of the said Bullaries of salt water in his demesne as of freehould for tearme of his naturall liffe with divers remainders on the last day of march in the third yeare of his ma[jes]ties Raigne of England and of no greater estate as he verilie taketh it and this he knoweth to be true by reason that he this depon[en]t was of counsell with the said Robte Wintour in makinge of one Indenture bearinge date about the tenth day of march in the said xlij[o] yeare of the Raigne of our said late Queene Eliz[abeth] whereby and by a fine and recoverie thereupon levied and suffered it is made or declared that the said Robte Wintour had as this depon[en]t taketh it an estate of and in one of the said five and twenty Bullaries in fee simple. And of and in the other foure and twenty Bullaries with the appurtenances the said Robte Wintour had an estate for tearme of his liffe with divers remainders over as by the said Indenture may appeare, whereunto this depon[en]t referreth himselfe for more certainty.

5 To the fifth inter[rogatory] he saith that over and besides the said Indenture mentioned in his answeare to the fourth inter[rogatory] he hath seene the indented Chirographe of the fine levied upon the said Indenture and hath likewise seene the Recoverie under the seale of the Court of common pleas suffered upon and according to the intent of the said Indenture and saith that the said fine to his now remembrance was levied of foure and twenty of those Bullaries in [illegible] Termino Trinitatis xlij[o] Elizabethe Regine And the Recoverie is Inrolled the same tearme as appeareth Rotulo xxxviij[o] of the said xxiiij[or] Bullaries And saith further That that Indenture in the fourth inter[rogatory] mentioned made about the tenth day of march in the said two and fortieth yeare of Queene Elizabeth was made Betweene Robte Wintour of Huddington Thomas Wintour second brother of the said Robte John Wintour youngest brother of the said Robte John Grant of Snitterfield in the county of Warwick and Edward Cookes of the middle Temple London gent on the one pte and John Talbott of Grafton in the said County of Worcester esquire and John Talbott of Longford in the Com[itatu] of Salop esquire on the other pte And saith he did see all the said pties hereunto seale and deliver and accept interchangeably the two ptes of the said indenture And that the same was so sealed delivered and accepted of about the end of march in the said two and fortieth yeare of the Raigne of the said late Queene Elizabeth or before the first day of Aprill in that xlij[o] yeare.

6 To the sixt inter[rogatory] this depon[en]t saith that at the time of the sealinge and delivery of the said Indenture he this depon[en]t did see the said Robte [illegible] deliver unto the said John Talbott of Longford one paire of gloves of the [illegible] for the [illegible] and [illegible] the signification or declaration in that Indenture expressed And [illegible] the said John Talbott of Longford then and there accept of the said gloves and [illegible].

7 To the seventh Interrogatory he this depon[en]t saith That in the said indenture there is some [illegible] or Condition contained to give [illegible] power or authority [illegible] limitinge revokinge or makinge void the uses in that indenture contained but saith that the said power [illegible] was not [illegible] of the said Robte Wintour but restrained and [illegible] that the said Robte Wintour could not [illegible] thereof without the consent of the said John Talbott of Grafton as this depon[en]t taketh it [illegible]

this image; he lives the backstairs life of a loner, on the fringe of society, difficult, cultured and superior, far removed from the materialistic, self-satisfied place-hunters he deceives in his love poems. But Donne did change. He took the path away from martyrdom, studied the religious controversy between Catholicism and the established church, and convinced himself that his spiritual and material interests were the same thing.

By 1610 he had written in favour of the oath of allegiance which James enforced on Catholics after the plot. In this work, entitled 'Pseudo-Martyr', Donne criticized those who preferred to die rather than change, though his private opinions about the oath of allegiance were very much more ambiguous. As Dean of St Paul's, one of the senior and most conspicuous figures of the established church, Donne gave the sermon on 'Gunpowder Day' 1622 'intended for Paul's Cross [a favourite location for official sermons], but by reason of the weather preached in the church'. In the sermon, he tells how the plotters would have turned Parliament from a hive producing the honey of benign legislation into a giant gun designed to shoot God (King James as God's representative) back at God in heaven. As with the oath of allegiance, it is doubtful whether Donne's private opinions about Parliament mirrored his public utterances. From a poet's point of view, however, the genuine element was the irresistibly vivid image of king, nobles, commons and people being shot out of an enormous artillery piece into the air. The imaginative possibilities of the poet's sermon allowed him to fantasize the destruction of a society which had compelled him to abandon his faith from the comfortable position of a favoured royal preacher.

Yet in the end the Gunpowder Plot did not succeed. It remains for us a fascinating piece of history, celebrated – and misunderstood – every autumn as an enduring part of national life. The real players, and their complex motives, belong to the shifting, uncertain world of the Jacobean court, vividly evoked by dramatists who saw the theatrical potential of its shadows and ambiguities. In the plotters' letters and testimonies, where wordplay and equivocation become strategies of survival, we begin to approach the hopes and fears of those who sought to reshape their country's destiny.

Epilogue

One of the reasons why the Gunpowder Plot attracts such controversy and so many conspiracy theories is that Catesby's choice of scheme and justification of it seem so inadequate to a modern reader. Why risk so much for so little? Why go to the trouble and hazard of blowing up the king and nobility in order to replace them with James's younger son or elder daughter and those lords who survived the blast? Catesby's reported contempt for the majority of the lords sounded genuine, but he was hardly planning social revolution. Were the plotters so desperate that they would really risk death for even a slim chance of interrupting an unending Protestant succession and an ever more hostile England?

Unlikely though it may seem, there is some evidence for this. Many of the plotters had already risked their lives in rebellion or fighting in the Low Countries; in the plot they were at least in command of their own forces, however small. Did they even deliberately court martyrdom? They certainly appeared dressed for it, in their finest clothes with their engraved swords and religiously embroidered scarves. Since the church taught that consequences of apostasy were worse than death, perhaps they really were 'sooner dead than changed'. On the other hand, many of the plotters were not from settled Catholic backgrounds; they were converts who had often lived in outward conformity for long periods. Thomas Wintour, for example, had apparently fought on both sides in the Low Countries, while Robert Catesby lived a life of quiet conformity until the death of his wife. Guy Fawkes adopted the religion of his stepfather, and John Wright, imprisoned as a precaution during Queen Elizabeth's illness in 1596, only converted to Catholicism in 1601. They were hardly models of simple religious loyalty, rather a group for whom religion was a badge of disaffection as well as its cause. Catesby, tired of Garnet's religious diplomacy, decided to take decisive action while the Jesuit was away on pilgrimage.

Though their own loyalties were complex and shifting, the plotters decided, and perhaps really believed, that the mass of people were a much simpler proposition. Given a decisive 'blow' and strong leadership, the people would throw off the new religion with a shrug and hail their saviours – elegantly dressed gentlemen of the old faith to whom they had temporarily closed their hearts – as model Englishmen, at the head rather than on the fringes of their society. The pursuit of self-interest was perhaps more deeply ingrained than the plotters would have liked to believe, not least in themselves. As we have seen, there were few players behind the plot whose loyalties were not questionable. The society that proved so hostile to the plotters was itself unsure of its own loyalties. James had invented and re-instated a whole layer of aristocracy and gentility to give him networks of patronage in his new kingdom, where he was widely accepted but lacked deep, socially rooted support. Beneath this tier, suitors followed their patrons not out of ancient loyalty but for what they could get.

The plotters, though they regarded the place-hunting, materialistic court with contempt, were an integral part of this culture. Thomas Wintour took Lord Monteagle as his patron when he needed him, but was ready to throw him off when he was rich enough to be 'his own man'; Northumberland suggested that Thomas Percy was simply biding his time with the earl in hope of supplanting him, as perhaps Northumberland was biding his time with the king. Loyalty to any principle or idea is very often difficult to detect. The plotters had looked to Spain partly because it promised to fill the gap in patronage left when the Earl of Essex fell from favour. No matter that Essex had been head of the anti-Spanish faction at court; one of his main objections to Cecil had been that he was pro-Spanish, and that he and most of the Privy Council were 'Spanish pensioners'. Waad wrote to Salisbury on 8 November 1605, informing him that Francis Tresham was one of this faction worth watching, in the full knowledge that Salisbury had been the best-paid Spanish pensioner in the country. Despite the plotters' despair of help from Spain after the peace treaty of 1604, it seems that Catesby still saw himself leading English soldiers in a Spanish army. He also exercised petty patronage of his own, like a nobleman, promising to take as a page the 'base boy' of Humphrey Littleton (brother of the conspirator Stephen Littleton, and the betrayer of Henry Garnet; he was himself executed at Worcester with Edward Oldcorne and John Wintour).

Against this background, had Catesby really believed that the Catholics would act uniformly, believing religious loyalty and self-interest were the same thing? Was he in this sense an anachronism? At the same time as he reported that the king and Salisbury were dead, Catesby reported that the Privy Council had ordered that the throats of all the English Catholics should be cut, a scare story taken from Catesby's childhood in the years before the defeat of the Armada. Would they stick together as a group as they must do in those circumstances, or had their motivations become more diverse and complex?

Parliament and the People

It is striking to a modern audience just how little attention was paid by the plotters or the government to the probable destruction of the House of Commons in the gunpowder explosion. We are accustomed to seeing the period around the Gunpowder Plot as the time of the great rise of the Commons in power and influence, from haggles over taxation late in Elizabeth's reign intensifying under the early Stuarts and ending inevitably in civil war. The documents of the plot show little sign of this. Both plotters and king believed government was about a few 'great men', and democracy was an equally alien concept to both. The 'principal commons' are a bit of an afterthought on the list of possible casualties. Sir William Waad as Lieutenant of the Tower reported the occasional spat between his office and that of the mayor and city of London, perhaps showing underlying hostility to ancient court privileges from a clear opposition group, which drew Waad's curse 'a pox on all offices and officers'.

Yet the possible loss of popular representation through parliamentary government was barely an issue in the Gunpowder Plot. This is not just striking in a modern context, but also given the fact that the English Civil War occurred less than 40 years after the plot. Then Catholics, including, with a nice dramatic irony, the descendants of the plotters, had little option but to side with the king. Perhaps the most telling moment of the Midlands rebellion was the plotters' reception at Lord Windsor's house, Hewell Grange, where they plundered weapons. As recounted by Robert Wintour's servant Thomas Maunder, they were looking for support and announcing they were for 'God and the Country' when 'one of the countrymen set his back to the wall and set his staff before him saying he was for King James for whom he would live and die and would not go against him'. Given the fluctuating loyalty of many of the players behind the plot, and the cavalier attitude of both the plotters and the government to popular opinion, such an overt demonstration of loyalty appears almost as inexplicable as it is touching. Guy Fawkes had reported to the Spanish court that popular opinion in England was so against their new foreign king that the country was ripe for rebellion. Later he was equally confident that if the plotters proclaimed themselves to have acted out of a desire to prevent union with Scotland, the popular acclamation would be such that a carefully introduced Catholic government would be welcomed as part of the deal. Both the plotters and the government believed that the success or failure of rebellion depended on great leadership and the people being borne along in its wake on an unstoppable historical tide. Yet this was not the case. The people, like the other players behind the plot, had their own motivations.

Chronology

1586

Henry Garnet arrives in England. Discovery of Babington Plot. Arrest of William Weston, Father Superior of the English Jesuit province. Garnet appointed Superior, begins to build on the network of Catholic safe houses established by Anne Vaux and others

1588

Spanish Armada sails to attack England; defeated

1596

Dangerous illness of Queen Elizabeth. Known malcontents, including John Wright, imprisoned as a precaution

1601

Rebellion and execution of the Earl of Essex. Francis Tresham, Robert Catesby, Lord Monteagle and the Wrights all involved in the plot

1603

Death of Elizabeth. Accession of James VI of Scotland to the English throne.

Main and Bye Plots combine priestly assassination of the king and the possibility of Spanish invasion

1604

Treaty of London ends war with Spain

1605

June

Henry Garnet leads several conspirators and their families on pilgrimage to Wales

July

Garnet hears of the plot in 'walking confession' from Oswald Tesimond, confessor to Robert Catesby

26 October; Saturday

Lord Monteagle receives an anonymous letter warning him to avoid attendance at Parliament. He reports this to the king and the Privy Council

Sir Thomas Edmondes, English ambassador to Flanders, reports from Brussels on English Catholic confidence and reported conversions in letters to Earl of Salisbury

27 October; Sunday

Plotters learn of the 'Monteagle letter' thanks to Thomas Wintour's connections with the Monteagle household. Catesby, Fawkes and Thomas Wintour staying at White Webbs, a house rented by Anne Vaux near Theobalds, Salisbury's house in Hertfordshire

30 October; Wednesday

Fawkes ventures out, unaware of discovery although other conspirators know of the letter, and finds the powder undisturbed

31 October; Thursday

The king returns to London from hunting. Thomas Wintour comes to London

1 November ; Friday

Thomas Wintour and Catesby accuse Tresham of having revealed the plot; his denials only half-convince. Tresham urges abandonment or at least postponement; believes the letter has achieved this. Tresham plans to be out of the country before anything happens

2 November; Saturday

Another letter about a plot to assassinate King James is 'found on the street'

Passport issued for Francis Tresham to travel for two years

3 November; Sunday

Percy stiffens the resolution of the conspirators and resolves to gauge official knowledge of the plot through his master, the Earl of Northumberland

4 November; Monday

Percy dines with Northumberland at Syon House

Initial search and the midnight raid on the vault. Fawkes arrested, gunpowder discovered

Percy and Catesby leave London

5 November; Tuesday

Thomas Wintour goes to Parliament on Tuesday morning to confirm the rumours of discovery, then rides north

Initial examination of 'John Johnson', Fawkes's alias

Proclamation issued for the apprehension of Thomas Percy. Percy reported escaping from London in all directions

Sir John Popham's investigations lead immediately to the core plotters

Rendezvous at Dunchurch; Catesby, Percy and the Wrights bring news of the arrest of Fawkes and the failure of the plot. Catesby begins to tell wild lies about the king's death and proposes open rebellion; the majority melt away

Horse-stealing raid on Warwick Castle

6 November; Wednesday

[Morning] 'Johnson' examined on Percy connection

James writes letter authorizing the torture of 'Johnson'

[Afternoon] 'Johnson' answers on Percy connection, yielding little

Sir John Popham revises his list of suspects, additions and omissions based on the confession of 'Johnson'

First reports of the Midlands rebellion

The king's daughter, Lady Elizabeth, removed to Coventry

Robert Wintour writes urgent letter, found later at Holbeach House

Sir Everard Digby writes to Henry Garnet at Coughton for pardon and support; does not receive it. Mary Digby, also at Coughton, overhears her husband's fate discussed

7 November; Thursday

Thomas Wintour absolved with Catesby at Huddington; picks up armour from Lord Windsor's and goes to Holbeach House

Gunpowder explosion at Holbeach stirs fears of divine disapproval. Mass desertions of rebel supporters

Proclamation against the rebels issued, countering rumours of the involvement of a foreign power

Salisbury's narrative of the plot is read alongside the confession in Parliament

Chamberlain writes to Carleton with news of the first 'Bonfire Night', (the burning of Sandys's books) and encloses copy of the 'Monteagle letter'

Catesby's Hillingdon house searched. Thomas Percy unsuccessfully sought there

8 November; Friday

[Morning] Siege of Holbeach House. Gentlemanly arrests and suspicious deaths of vital witnesses including Percy, Catesby and John and Christopher Wright, all mortally wounded. Ambrose Rookwood and Thomas Wintour captured

Third proclamation aims to set rebel against rebel by singling out Percy on the day he is mortally wounded at Holbeach. Percy is taken prisoner; dies on 9 November

Percy 'seen' riding towards Rochester

Sir William Waad notes Francis Tresham and other 'Spanish

pensioners' in London as being worth watching. Tresham is not formally connected by the authorities with the plot until implicated by Fawkes on 9 November

Fawkes's next confession names conspirators and details the development of the plot – but is rendered superfluous by the information flooding in from Holbeach.

Digby rides away from Holbeach before the siege on the pretext of getting reinforcements; he is cornered by a posse while trying to find someone of rank to accept his surrender

Lord Montagu begins a conspiratorial correspondence with his father-in-law the Earl of Dorset, Lord Treasurer

Fawkes makes declaration to Salisbury with failing signature

11 NOVEMBER; Monday

Use of White Webbs, Enfield Chase, a safe house for priests including Henry Garnet, Father Superior of the Jesuit Mission in England, is revealed

King James sends an account of the plot to his brother-in-law Christian IV of Denmark. The rebellion is remarkable for the lack of force needed to suppress it and the absence of popular support

12 NOVEMBER; Tuesday

Warwickshire prisons overflowing with recusants in the wake of the Midlands rebellion; reports of patchy law enforcement, local loyalties and alliances

Catesby household at Ashby searched

Search of the Vaux home at Harrowden begins and lasts nine days

Survivors of Holbeach House siege brought to London

13–30 NOVEMBER

Declaration of Francis Tresham

Plot reported as a fable in France

Further reports emerge of seige of Holbeach, 'the multitude beat the grievously wounded traitors, Catesby, Percy and the two Wrights, beyond hope of recovery'

Lords Mordaunt and Montagu sent to the Tower

Reports of Earl of Northumberland being a focus for discontent in the summer

Ports (closed since 5 November) re-opened by order of the Privy Council – 'The plot being now thoroughly discovered and the principal offenders in the hands of his Majesty.'

Fawkes's further declaration strongly suggests Tresham as author of the 'Monteagle letter' as he was 'exceeding earnest' to warn him; backs nobles' stories regarding absence from Parliament

Exhumation and quartering of the conspirators who died at Holbeach

Second search at Catesby's Hillingdon house; his goods confiscated

Sir Richard Walsh reports seizing the arms of John Talbot of Grafton, searching Huddington Court and seizing Thomas Wintour's papers.

Proclamation issued for the apprehension of Robert Wintour and Stephen Littleton

Permission granted to sheriffs enabling them to pursue rebels into neighbouring counties – rather after the event

Official chronology of the meetings and proceedings of the plotters compiled

Circumstantial evidence links the plotters with the Jesuits

Attempt made to establish a link between Robert Wintour and the Countess of Shrewsbury

Sir Edward Coke examines Northumberland

Thomas Wintour makes a confession, annotated by the king

Comfortable accommodation at the Tower is over-subscribed, causing difficulty for Sir William Waad

Northumberland joins the other lords in the Tower, exacerbating problems with appropriate accommodation

Examination of Francis Tresham; Monteagle's name pasted out again

Examination of Robert Keyes reveals Catesby's contempt for the Lords

Garnett writes from hiding at Hindlip House to protest his innocence to the Privy Council

DECEMBER

Further enquiry made about the possibility of a northern rebellion, including a Spanish regiment led by Catesby

Examinations of Sir Everard Digby and Ambrose Rookwood

Mary Digby's plea of innocency and for her property; complaints made of the corruption of the law officers who pocket the proceeds

Examination of Thomas Bate

Anonymous letter warning of assassination attempts against Salisbury

Discovery of the priest hole at Huddington House

More information on Fawkes's background supplied by Sir William Waad

Sir Walter Raleigh closely monitored in the Tower; his renewed boldness taken as a sign that he is preparing to lead an anti-government party. Raleigh's wild denials of involvement with inside information 'fitter to be related than written'

Circumstantial evidence emerges from Salisbury's spies about papal backing for the plot

Examination of Francis Tresham

Monteagle's debt to Percy uncovered – offers a further reason why Percy might wish to preserve him. Reference to Percy's two wives – suspected of bigamy

Northumberland recalls his conversation with Percy on 4 November

Waad reports Tresham's death in the Tower

1606

JANUARY

Sir Thomas Edmondes reports to Salisbury that after initial sympathy for a fellow monarch, Spanish court now fears reprisals against English Catholics

Further examination of Guy Fawkes; negotiations with Rome

Arrest of Robert Wintour and Stephen Littleton at Hagley in Worcestershire

Humphrey Littleton, brother of Stephen, reveals that Henry Garnet is hiding at Hindlip House

Proclamation issued for the detention of Gerard, Garnet and Tesimond

Examination of Robert Wintour

Examination of Stephen Littleton, who had 'laid hid in barns and poor men's houses'

Hindlip House searched; Nicholas Owen and Ralph Ashley discovered

Guy Fawkes, Thomas and Robert Wintour, Robert Keyes, John Grant, Thomas Bate, Ambrose Rookwood and Sir Everard Digby are finally tried in Westminster Hall on 27 January. Fawkes and Robert Wintour reported to regret the opportunity to justify their actions to the world

Sentence against Sir Everard Digby; pleads guilty. Sentence against Thomas Wintour, Fawkes, Keyes, Robert Wintour, Grant, Rookwood and Bate; they plead not guilty. Fawkes complains that the indictment can be denied due to untrue elements

Summary execution of the aiders and abetters of Littleton and Robert Wintour; those who might provide further information are spared

Garnet and Oldcorne emerge from Hindlip House after eight days in the priest's hole

Digby, Robert Wintour, Grant and Bate executed at the west end of St Paul's in London on 30 January

Thomas Wintour, Rookwood, Keyes

1606

and Fawkes executed outside Westminster Hall on 31 January

February

Examination of Lords Stourton and Mordaunt for their non-attendance in Parliament

Thomas Phelippes protests his innocence to Salisbury. Unclear whether he was brought in by the government on a trumped-up charge to forge Garnet's letters

Garnet brought to London from Worcestershire – slowly, because of his physical weakness

Edward Oldcorne and Garnet committed to the Gatehouse prison in London

Mary Digby sues to be allowed to buy her unsold goods back, and for copies of the inventory of goods sent to the Exchequer

Interrogatories put to Garnet and Oldcorne; their conversations reported, but their testimonies are contradictory

Garnet moved from the Gatehouse prison to the Tower

Lord Cobham in the Tower thinks the Gunpowder Plot crisis has subsided sufficiently to renew his suit to Salisbury (his brother-in-law) for release from imprisonment on another charge

First of Garnet's letters written in orange juice, ('invisible' ink), intercepted and deciphered

Garnet writes on the lawfulness of blowing up Parliament

Garnet asserts 'They have nothing against me but presumptions'; admits telling less than the truth about White Webbs and his connection to the plotters

Confession of Nicholas Owen; he admits nothing

Submission of expenses claim of 23*s* 9*d* for setting Catesby's and Percy's heads on iron spikes

March

Final examination and death of Nicholas Owen

Further 'orange juice' letters from Garnet to Anne Vaux intercepted

Oldcorne contradicts Garnet again about the use of White Webbs

Oldcorne implicates Monteagle; subsequently made to qualify his statement

Sir Thomas Edmondes writes to Salisbury of Catesby's plans to be lieutenant-colonel of a Spanish regiment

Salisbury writes to Edmondes that Garnet guilty 'ex ore proprio' of concealing treason

Garnet's declaration of his proceedings in the plot, endorsed by Salisbury; 'Forbidden by the K[ing] to be given in evidence'

Three lords (Mordaunt, Stourton and Montagu) tried in court of Star Chamber, not at common law

Examination of Anne Vaux

Garnet testifies he knew of the plot in July 1605 'under the seal of the confessional'

Northumberland writes to Salisbury, still exercising patronage and administering his estates

Intense questioning of Garnet and Oldcorne; Popham displays accumulated evidence of Garnet's guilt

Initial commission issued for the trial of Garnet

Persistent rumours of other planned plots

'Orange juice' letter from Anne Vaux to Garnet declares that life without him 'is not life but death'

Rumour that James has been killed hunting at Woking becomes serious enough to need a proclamation to refute

Indictment of Henry Garnet

Francis Tresham's retraction (examined posthumously) of his implication of Garnet

Anne Vaux writes of Garnet's attempts to restrain the plotters.

1606 Garnet gives evidence of papal directions on the inadmissibility of a Protestant monarch

Chamberlain reports that Garnet will be arraigned at Guildhall; claims that he will be too drunk to give evidence

James I gives instructions to Coke via Salisbury on the conduct of Garnet's trial

Garnet pleads not guilty, but is sentenced to death

April

Theological questioning of Garnet in Latin

Garnet writes fifth 'orange juice' letter to Vaux, envisaging them together in heavenly tabernacle in his dreams

Official reports of Garnet's trial issued; Chamberlain describes it in letters

Garnet writes to Anne Vaux again with a view to posterity, describing her place with the Jesuits

Garnet writes declaration to the king – very different to his thoughts to Vaux

Garnet induced to write to the 'captive' Tesimond

Contradictory declarations of Garnet drawn from him 'to disclose his hypocrisy'

Garnet's obvious contradictions excused as evidence of torture by apologists in Flanders. Rumours begin that Nicholas Owen died of torture, not suicide

Examination of Warwickshire recusants reveals ignorance as much as confirmed faith: they have 'not been to church these forty years, brought up in the old law'

Edward Oldcorne, John Wintour (brother of Robert and Thomas) and Humphrey Littleton (brother of Stephen) executed at Worcester

Garnet's last letter to Anne Vaux reports Oldcorne's execution

Salisbury recommends to Edmondes that Garnet's execution should be deferred to avoid 'holy week, as they call it'

Garnet continues policy of equivocation, discrediting his own evidence

May

Garnet's execution deferred from May Day for fear of disturbance

Garnet executed in St Paul's churchyard on 3 May. His 'portrait' on the 'miraculous straw' becomes an object of veneration among English Catholics

Reports from Brussels of Catholic propaganda after Garnet's execution

June–August

Proclamation issued that all Jesuits should leave the country

Fresh plots are hatched by Baldwin and others in Brussels; plots made against Salisbury's life

Secular clergy and lay Catholics dissociate from the Jesuits who are blamed for the treason

Declaration that proofs of James's pre-succession promises of toleration towards English Catholics are to be published

Interrogatories to the Earl of Northumberland focus upon his conduct towards Thomas Percy and the trust reposed in him

Countess of Northumberland writes to Salisbury about her husband's coming trial

Trial of Northumberland begins in Star Chamber. Northumberland is imprisoned for life for misprision of treason (he is released fifteen years later)

Lord Stourton writes unsuccessful plea for liberty to Salisbury from the Tower. (Lord Montagu will be released from the Tower in 1611 after a payment of £6000, enabling him to avoid the oath of allegiance and in lieu of recusancy fines)

A Note on Sources

Many of the documents highlighted in this book are held by the National Archives. The Domestic State Papers for the period [SP 14] contain an enormous amount of material including the 'Gunpowder Plot Book' [SP 14/216], a collection of over two hundred documents including the Monteagle letter and many of the confessions and examinations taken after the discovery of the plot. A document described as 'calendared' has had an estimated date assigned to it in the National Archives' catalogue.

I have also made use of less well known sources such as Exchequer: King's Remembrancer: Depositions taken by Commission [E 134], and Exchequer: King's Remembrancer: Special Commissions of Inquiry [E 178], now well described in the National Archives' online catalogue

www.catalogue.nationalarchives.gov.uk/default.asp

There are, of course, many relevant sources in other archives, the most prominent being the Earl of Salisbury's own papers at Hatfield House, some very similar in character to those preserved at the National Archives. They are available in published form in the Historical Manuscripts Commission's [HMC] *Calendar of Salisbury (Cecil) MSS (1870–1976)*. The papers of the Percy family, Dukes of Northumberland at Alnwick Castle, as described in the Appendix to HMC's *Third Report* (1872), include private papers of Henry Percy, Earl of Northumberland, from the time of the plot.

The Tresham family papers now at the British Library [Additional Manuscripts 39828–38] also published by HMC, *Various Collections III (1904),* include Sir Thomas Tresham's less than flattering assessment of Anne Vaux in the summer of 1599 and Francis Tresham's bleak appraisal of the worth of Robert Catesby's promises in early 1604.

Other relevant collections include the papers of the Digby family of Gayhurst, held by Buckinghamshire Record Office, which shed further light on Mary Digby's attempts to obtain the restoration of her estates after the death of Sir Everard Digby, and Catesby documents among the Ashley family papers at Northamptonshire Record Office. These include a copy of the marriage settlement of Robert Catesby on Katherine Leigh in 1592 and other deeds associated with the marriage.

Further information about these and other collections is available in The National Register of Archives, the central collecting point for information about manuscript sources for British history outside the public records. The indexes can be searched online at

www.nra.nationalarchives.gov.uk/nra/.

Further Reading

The Gunpowder Plot has spawned an enormous number of books, many controversial and polemical. Below is a short list of publications which make the original sources most accessible.

D. Jardine, *Criminal Trials* (Nattali and Bond, London, 1846). Supplies copious illustrations of the important periods of English history during the the reigns of Queen Elizabeth and King James I to which is added a narrative of the Gunpowder Plot

J. F. Larkin and P. L. Hughes (eds.), *Stuart Royal Proclamations* (Clarendon Press, Oxford, 1973).

N. E. McClure, *The Letters of John Chamberlain* (The American Philosophical Society, Philadelphia, 1939).

M. Nicholls, *Investigating Gunpowder Plot* (Manchester University Press, Manchester, 1991).

O. Tesimond, *The Gunpowder Plot: The Narrative of Oswald Tesimond Alias Greenway* translated from the Italian of the Stonyhurst manuscript, edited and annotated by Francis Edwards (Folio Society, 1973).

Index

[Page numbers shown in *italics* refer to illustrations]

Author's Acknowledgements

I should acknowledge my debt to Professor John Carey for his observations on John Donne's art and apostasy and thank him for lectures which nudged me towards history from literature.

I would also like to thank the following for their constructive advice and practical suggestions: Catherine Bradley, Jane Crompton, Karen Grannum, Melinda Haunton, Alfred Symons, Ken Wilson; and Sarah Travers for 'Brimstone and Treason'.

Picture acknowledgements

p. 7 British Library; p. 11 James I: Galleria degli Uffizi, Florence, Italy / Bridgeman Art Library; View of London: Guildhall Library, Corporation of London, UK / Bridgeman Art Library; p. 14 Galleria degli Uffizi, Florence, Italy / Bridgeman Art Library; p. 19 Rijksmuseum, Amsterdam, Holland / Bridgeman Art Library; p. 27 Vintner smoking pipe (right): Stapleton Collection, UK / Bridgeman Art Library; Portrait of Henry Howard (left): Private Collection / Bridgeman Art Library; p. 31 Private Collection © Richard Philp, London / Bridgeman Art Library; p. 36 © Guildhall Library, Corporation of London, UK / Bridgeman Art Library; p. 46 © Yale Center for British Art, Paul Mellon Collection, USA / Bridgeman Art Library; p. 50 © Rushton Hall; p. 56 Private Collection / Bridgeman Art Library; p. 67 Princess Elizabeth: National Maritime Museum, London, UK / Bridgeman Art Library; The Tower of London: Private Collection / Bridgeman Art Library; The Browne Brothers: © Burghley House Collection, Lincolnshire, UK / Bridgeman Art Library; p. 71 National Maritime Museum, London, UK/Bridgeman Art Library; p. 79 Private Collection / Bridgeman Art Library; p. 82 Stapleton Collection, UK/ Bridgeman Art Library; p. 102 © Burghley House Collection, Lincolnshire, UK/Bridgeman Art Library; p. 124 Private Collection / Bridgeman Art Library; p. 132 © Lambeth Palace Library, London, UK / Bridgeman Art Library; p. 135 Portrait of Sir Robert Cecil (top right): Private Collection / Bridgeman Art Library; Edward Coke (bottom left): © collection of the Earl of Leicester, Holkham Hall, Norfolk / Bridgeman Art Library; p. 139 Private Collection / Bridgeman Art Library; p. 149 Private Collection / Bridgeman Art Library; p. 158 © NTPL/Andrew Butler; p. 163 © collection of the Earl of Leicester, Holkham Hall, Norfolk / Bridgeman Art Library.

All document images are from the National Archives:

p. 11 Document: TNA: PRO SP 14/216/17; p. 22; p. 27 Document: TNA: PRO SP 14/216/2; p. 32; p. 35; p. 38; p. 39; p. 41; p. 42; p. 43; p. 47; p. 51; p. 53; p. 55; p. 58; p. 61; p. 63; p. 64; p. 67 Document: TNA: PRO SP 14/216/54; p. 74; p. 80; p. 83; p. 84; p. 87; p. 91; p. 95; p. 96; p. 97; p. 99; pp. 104–105; p. 107; p. 109; p. 111; p. 115; p. 118; p. 120; p. 123; p. 126; p. 130; p. 131; p. 135 Henry Garnet (top left): TNA: PRO SP 14/216/pt2; Document: TNA: PRO SP 14/20/39; p. 141; p. 142; p. 145 (14/216/pt2); p. 147; p. 150; p. 154; p. 159; p. 160; p. 164; p. 167; p. 170; p. 171 TNA: PRO (14/216/pt2); p. 175.